EASY GUITAR WITH NOTES & TAB

CHART HITS
OF 2017–2018

ISBN 978-1-5400-2327-8

7777 W. BLUEMOUND RD. P.O. BOX 13819 MILWAUKEE, WI 53213

Visit Hal Leonard Online at
www.halleonard.com

STRUM AND PICK PATTERNS

This chart contains the suggested strum and pick patterns that are referred to by number at the beginning of each song in this book. The symbols ⊓ and ∨ in the strum patterns refer to down and up strokes, respectively. The letters in the pick patterns indicate which right-hand fingers play which strings.

p = thumb
i = index finger
m = middle finger
a = ring finger

For example; Pick Pattern 2
is played: thumb - index - middle - ring

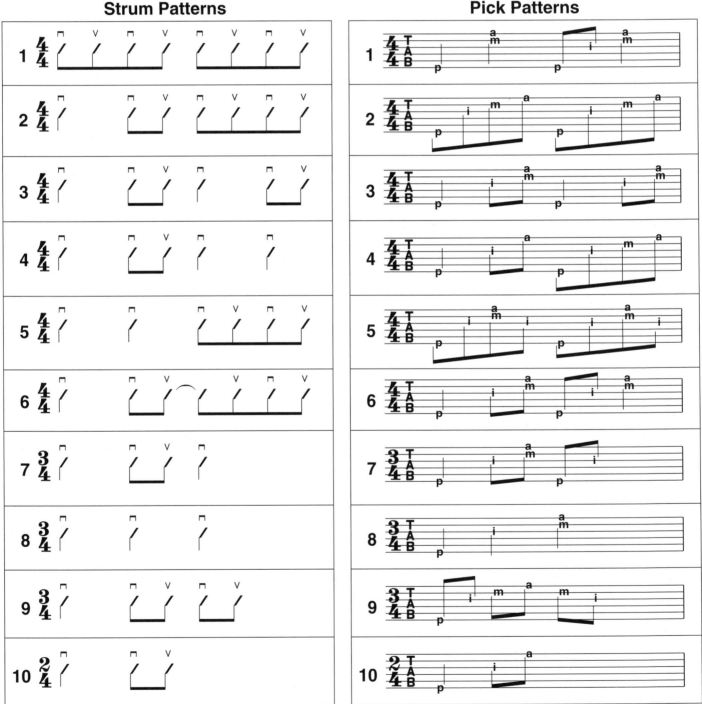

You can use the 3/4 Strum and Pick Patterns in songs written in compound meter (6/8, 9/8, 12/8, etc.).
For example, you can accompany a song in 6/8 by playing the 3/4 pattern twice in each measure.
The 4/4 Strum and Pick Patterns can be used for songs written in cut time (¢) by doubling the note time values in the patterns. Each pattern would therefore last two measures in cut time.

CONTENTS

Dear Hate

Words and Music by Maren Morris, Tom Douglas and David Hodges

*Capo II

Strum Pattern: 2, 3
Pick Pattern: 4

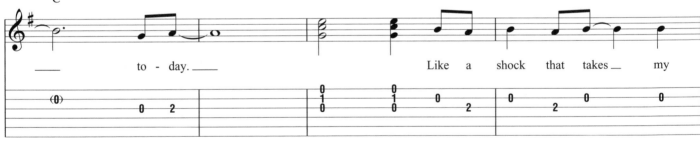

*Optional: To match recording, place capo at 2nd fret.

I'm a-fraid ___ that ___ we just ___ might drown. 2. Dear ___

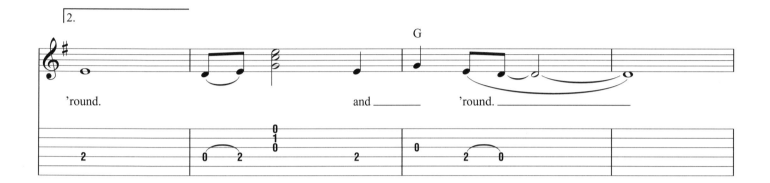

'round. and _____ 'round. _____

𝄋 Chorus

You were (1., 2.) there in the gar - den like a
(3.) there in the gar - den when I

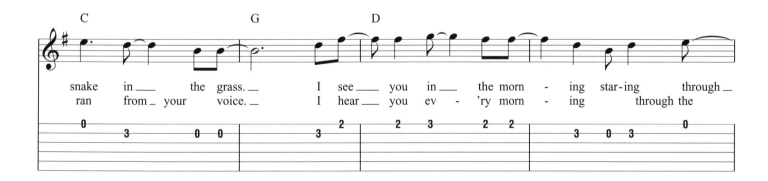

snake in ___ the grass. ___ I see ___ you in ___ the morn - ing star-ing through ___
ran from ___ your voice. ___ I hear ___ you ev - 'ry morn - ing through the

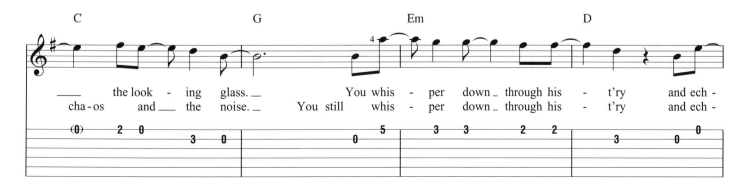

___ the look - ing glass. ___ You whis - per down ___ through his - t'ry and ech -
cha - os and ___ the noise. ___ You still whis - per down ___ through his - t'ry and ech -

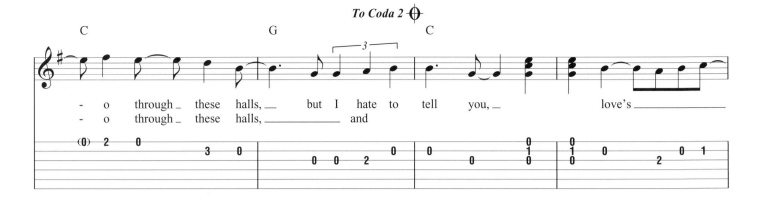

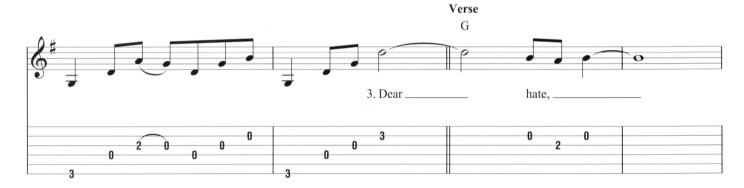

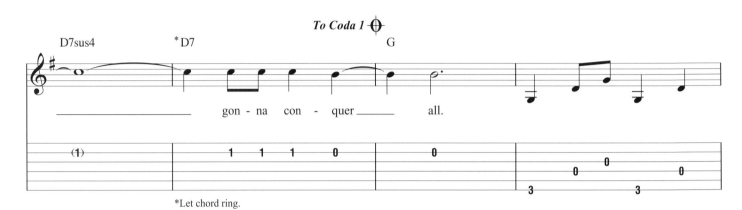

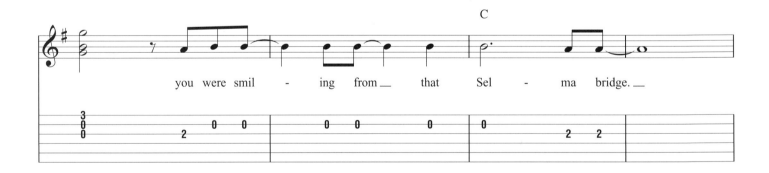

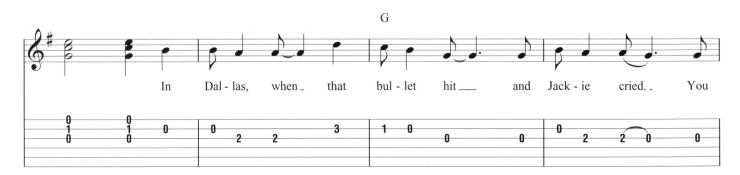

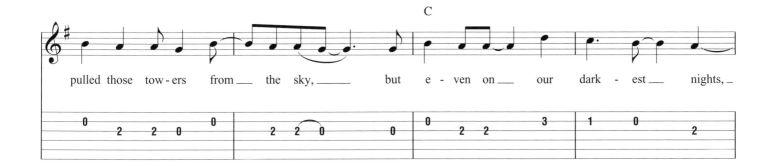

pulled those tow-ers from _ the sky, _ but e-ven on _ our dark-est _ nights, _

D.S. al Coda 1

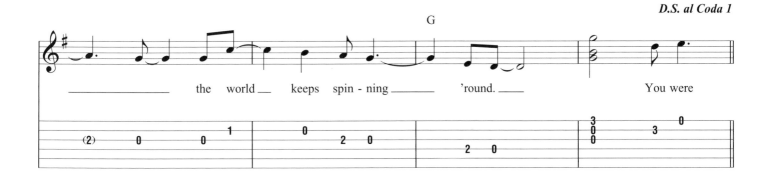

_ the world _ keeps spin-ning _ 'round. _ You were

⌖ Coda 1

Interlude

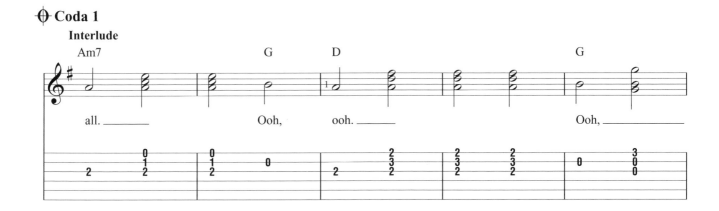

all. _ Ooh, ooh. _ Ooh, _

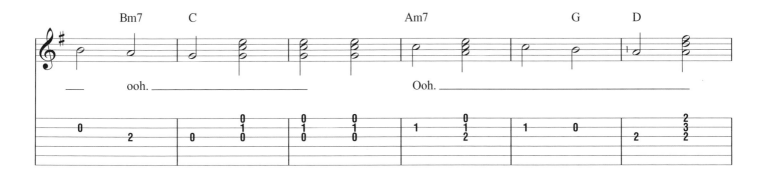

_ ooh. _ Ooh.

Verse

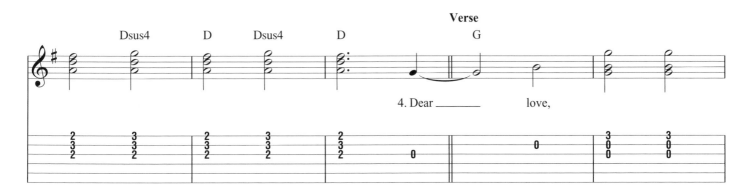

4. Dear _ love,

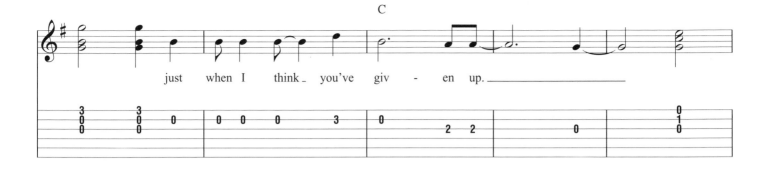

just when I think _ you've giv - en up. _____

D.S. al Coda 2

You were

⊕ Coda 2

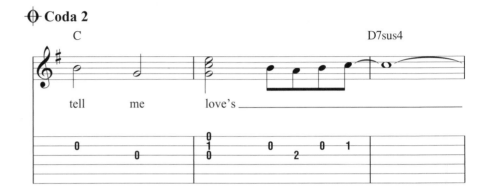

tell me love's _____

Outro

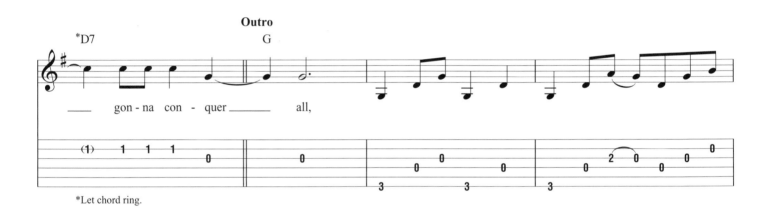

____ gon - na con - quer ____ all,

*Let chord ring.

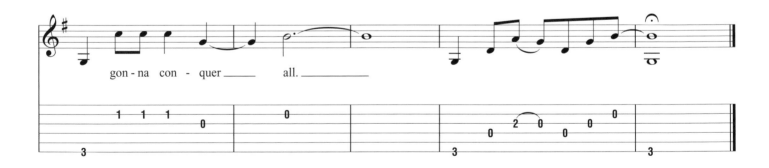

gon - na con - quer ____ all. _____

Additional Lyrics

2. Dear hate, well, you sure are colorblind.
   Your kiss is the cruelest kind.
   You could poison any mind, just look at mine.
   Don't know how this world keeps spinning 'round and 'round.

Greatest Love Story

Words and Music by Brandon Lancaster

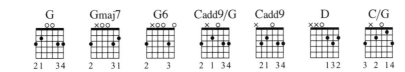

*Capo III

Strum Pattern: 3, 4
Pick Pattern: 4, 5

Intro
Moderately slow, in 2

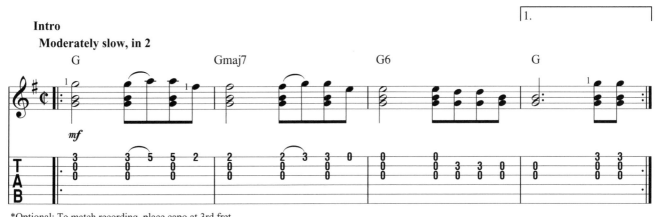

*Optional: To match recording, place capo at 3rd fret.

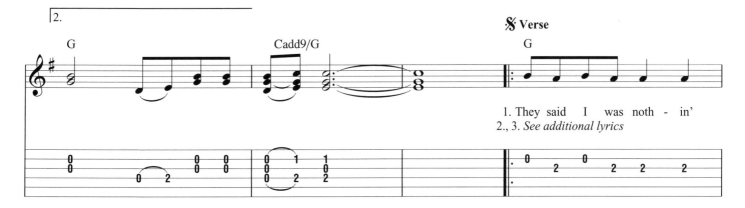

1. They said I was noth - in'
2., 3. *See additional lyrics*

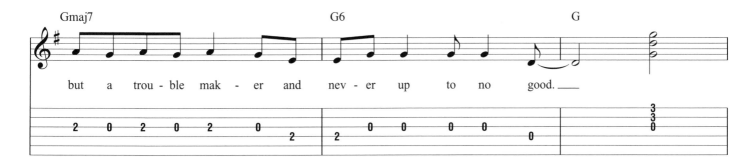

but a trou - ble mak - er and nev - er up to no good. ___

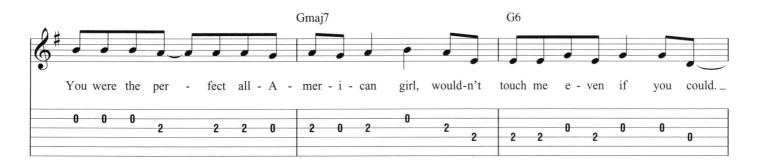

You were the per - fect all - A - mer - i - can girl, would-n't touch me e - ven if you could. ___

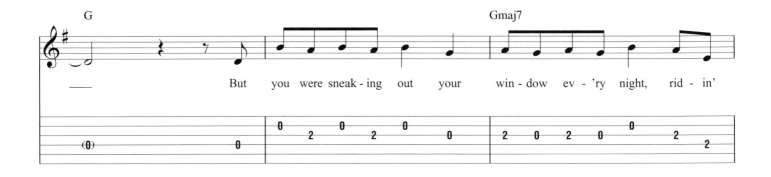

But you were sneak-ing out your win-dow ev-'ry night, rid-in'

shot-gun in my car. ___ We go to the riv-er and find ___ us a spot and we

3rd time, To Coda ⊕

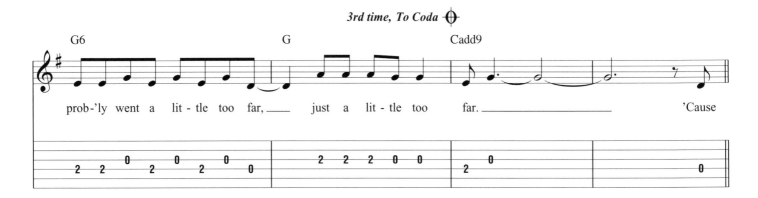

prob-'ly went a lit-tle too far, ___ just a lit-tle too far. _____ 'Cause

Chorus

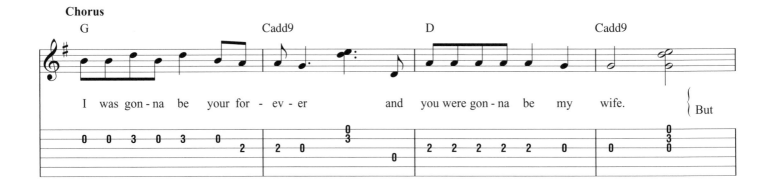

I was gon-na be your for-ev-er and you were gon-na be my wife. {But

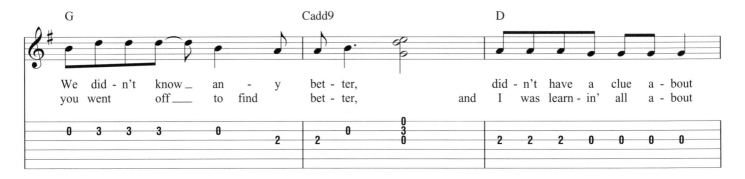

We did-n't know ___ an - y bet-ter, did-n't have a clue a-bout
you went off ___ to find bet-ter, and I was learn-in' all a-bout

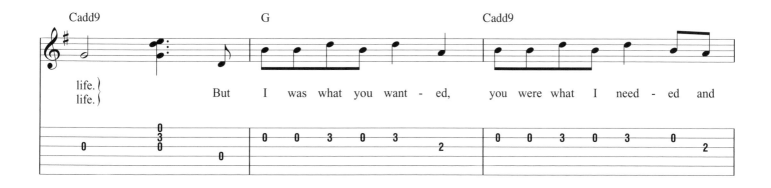

life. }
life. }

But I was what you want - ed, you were what I need - ed and

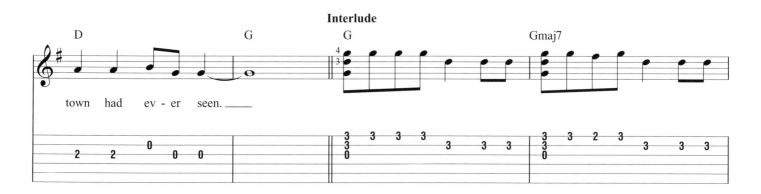

we could meet in ___ be - tween. ___ We were gon - na be the great - est love sto - ry this

Interlude

town had ev - er seen. ___

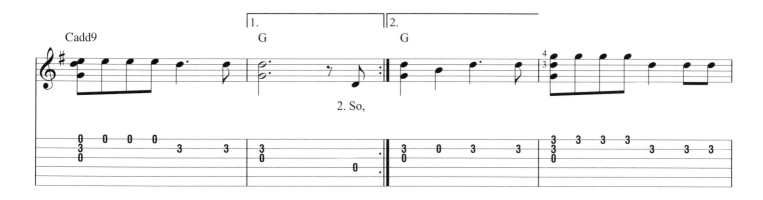

2. So,

D.S. al Coda

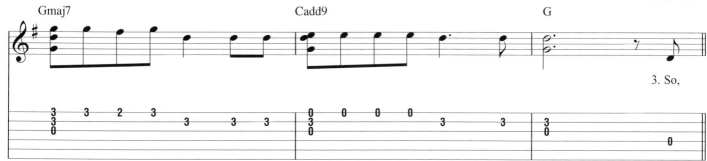

3. So,

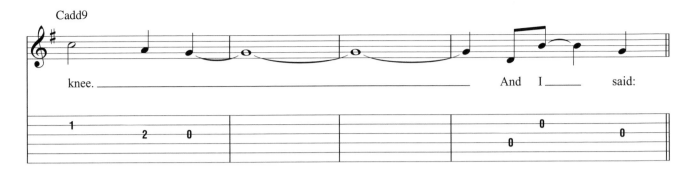

⊕ Coda

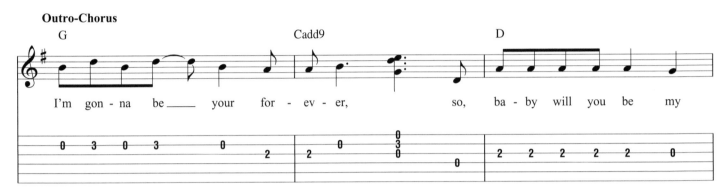

knee. _____ And I _____ said:

Outro-Chorus

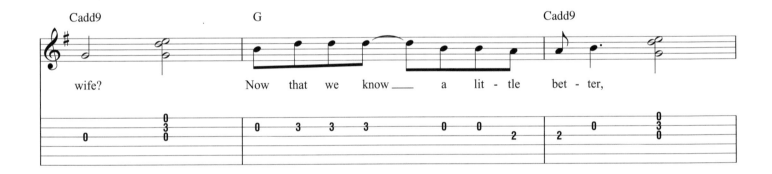

I'm gon - na be ____ your for - ev - er, so, ba - by will you be my

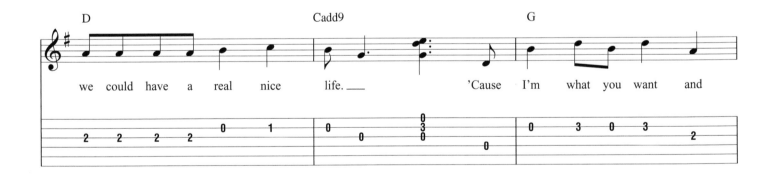

wife? Now that we know ___ a lit - tle bet - ter,

we could have a real nice life. ___ 'Cause I'm what you want and

you're what I need, so let's meet in ___ be - tween. ___

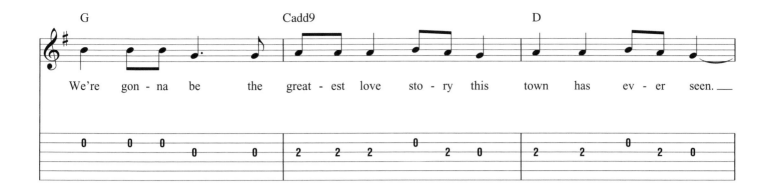

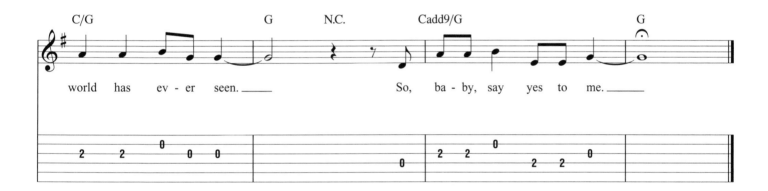

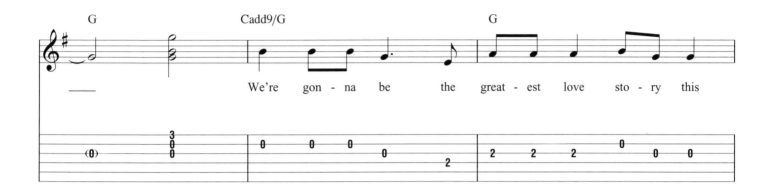

Additional Lyrics

2. So, you went off to college and I got a job. I was working that nine to five.
   Dreamin' of the days when you were in my arms, I had never felt so alive.
   I spent my days workin', spent my nights drinkin', howlin' at the moon.
   Screamin' for the days when you were comin' back. No, couldn't come too soon,
   Couldn't come too soon when...

3. So, you came back after a long four years. Your college boyfriend didn't work out.
   So, we went out for a couple of drinks to find out who we are now.
   Sure, we changed, but way deep down you had the same old feelings for me.
   I went to the store and bought you a ring and I got down on one knee,
   Down on one knee.

Feel It Still

Words and Music by John Gourley, Zach Carothers, Jason Sechrist, Eric Howk, Kyle O'Quin, Brian Holland, Freddie Gorman, Georgia Dobbins, Robert Bateman, William Garrett, John Hill and Asa Taccone

*Optional: To match recording, place capo at 4th fret.

*2nd time, N.C. next 2 meas.

reb - el just for kicks, now.) Give in to that eas - y liv - ing; good-bye to my hopes and dreams, __

__ start flip - ping for my en - e - mies. __ Or we could

wait un - til the walls come down. __ (Ooh, __ I'm a reb - el just for kicks, now.) It's

time to give a lit - tle to the kids in the mid - dle, but, oh, ___ un - til ___ it falls, __

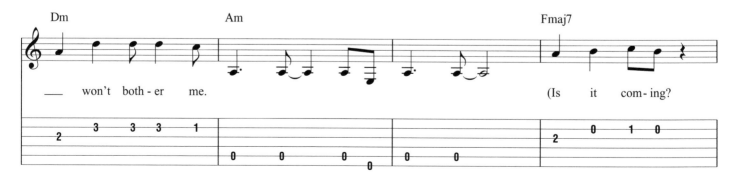

__ won't both - er me. (Is it com - ing?

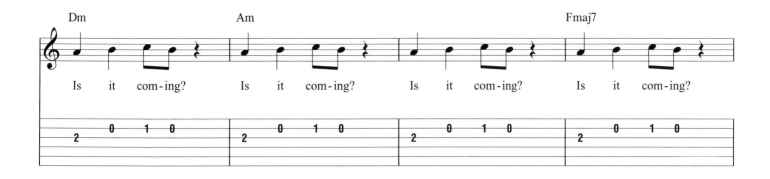

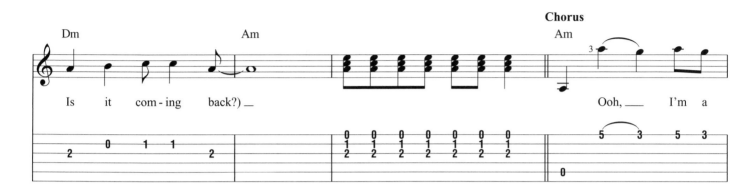

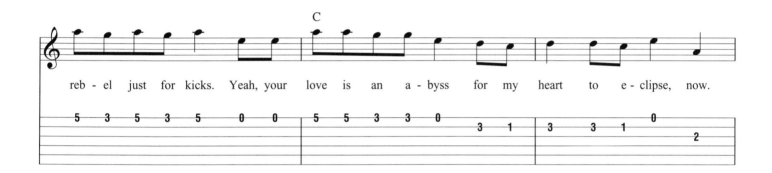

Havana

Words and Music by Camila Cabello, Louis Bell, Pharrell Williams, Adam Feeney, Ali Tamposi, Brian Lee, Andrew Wotman, Brittany Hazzard, Jeffery Lamar Williams and Brandon Perry

*Optional: To match recording, place capo at 3rd fret.

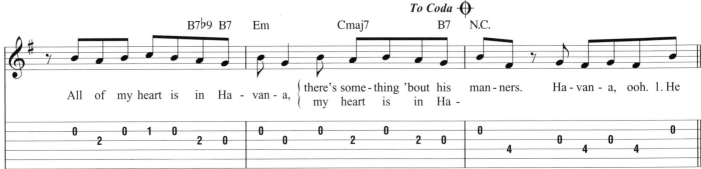

Verse

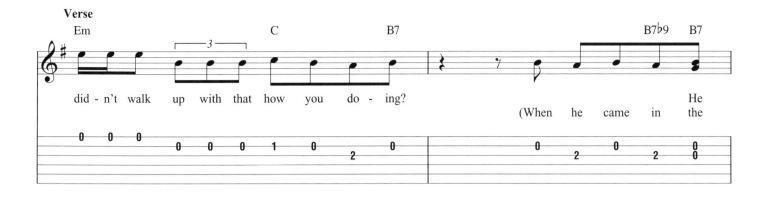

did-n't walk up with that how you do-ing?   He
                                                                              (When he came in the

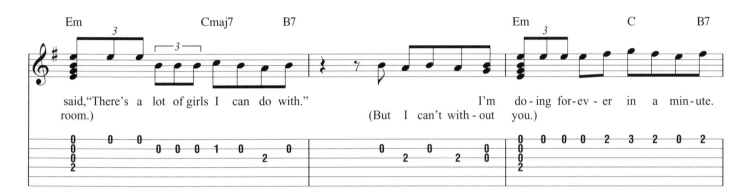

said, "There's a lot of girls I can do with."   I'm do-ing for-ev-er in a min-ute.
room.)   (But I can't with-out you.)

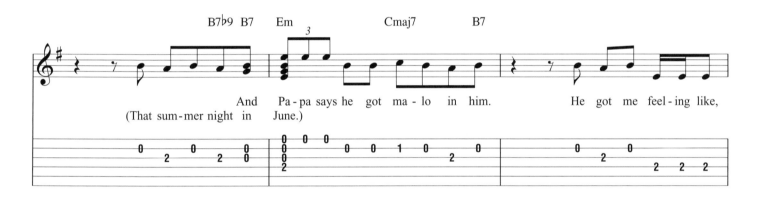

                    And Pa-pa says he got ma-lo in him.   He got me feel-ing like,
(That sum-mer night in June.)

ooh. _____   I knew it when I met him, I loved him when I

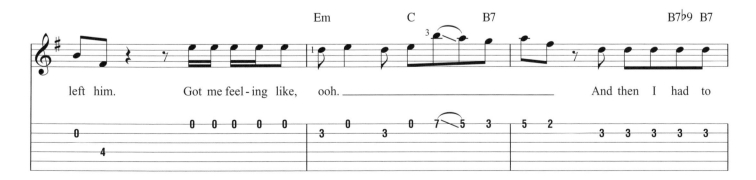

left him.   Got me feel-ing like, ooh. _____ And then I had to

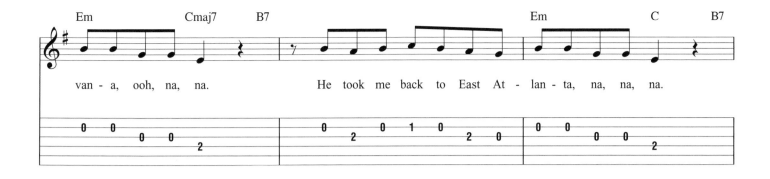

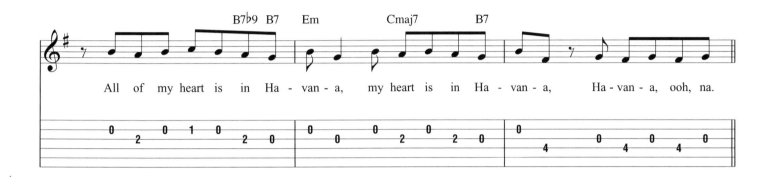

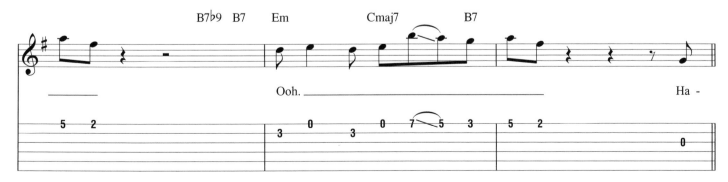

Outro-Chorus

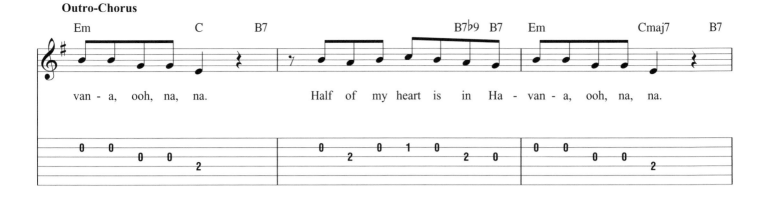

van - a, ooh, na, na.   Half of my heart is in Ha - van - a, ooh, na, na.

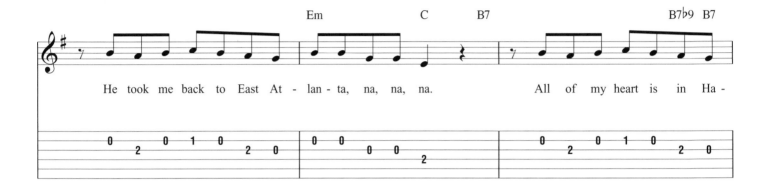

He took me back to East At - lan - ta, na, na, na.   All of my heart is in Ha -

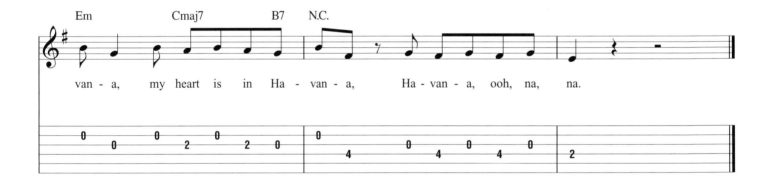

van - a, my heart is in Ha - van - a, Ha - van - a, ooh, na, na.

Additional Lyrics

2. Jeffery.
   Just graduated, fresh on campus, mmm.
   Fresh out East Atlanta with no manners, damn.
   Fresh out East Atlanta.
   Bump on her bumper like a traffic jam (jam).
   Hey, I was quick to pay that girl like Uncle Sam. (Here you go, ay.)
   Back it on me, shawty cravin' on me.
   Get to diggin' on me (on me).
   She waited on me. (Then what?)
   Shawty cakin' on me, got the bacon on me. (Wait up.)
   That is history in the makin' on me (on me).
   Point blank, close range, that be.
   If it cost a million, that's me (that's me).
   I was gettin' mula, man, they feel me.

Meant to Be

Words and Music by Bleta Rexha, Josh Miller, Tyler Hubbard and David Garcia

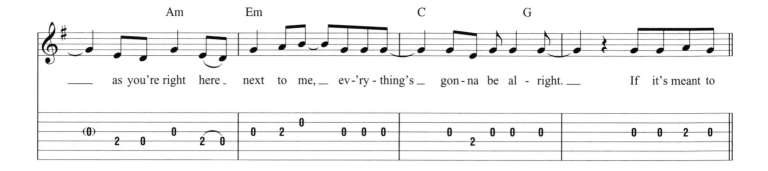

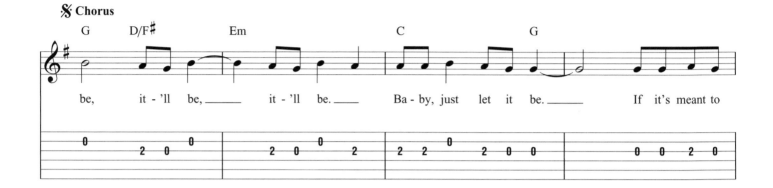

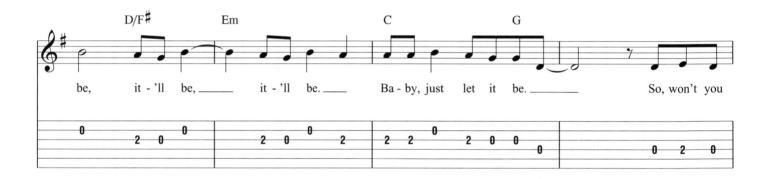

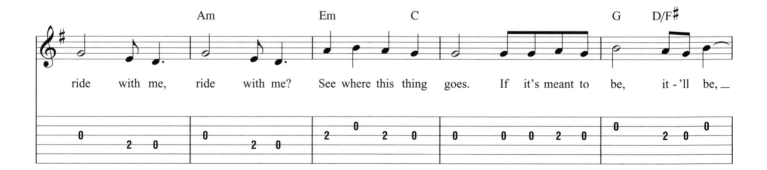

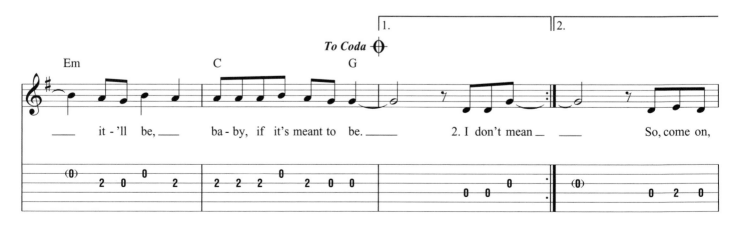

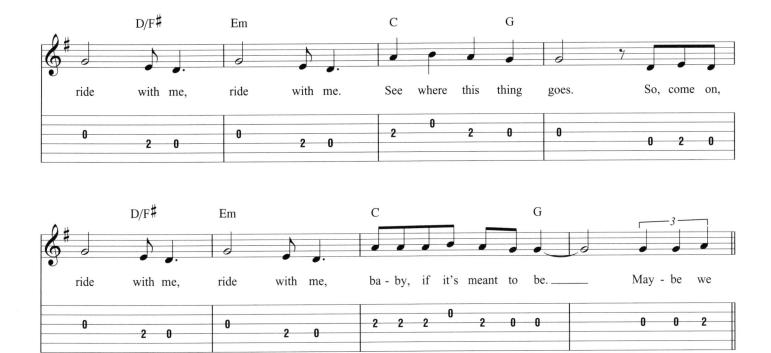

Bridge

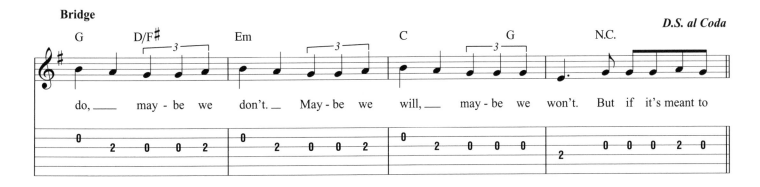

D.S. al Coda

Coda

Outro

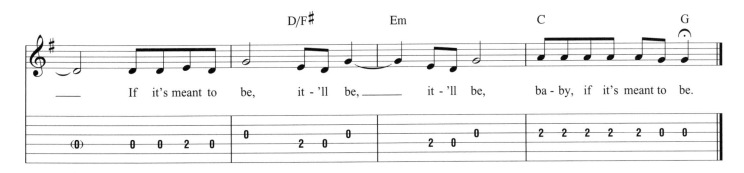

Additional Lyrics

2. I don't mean to be so uptight, but my heart's been hurt a couple times
   By a couple guys that didn't treat me right. I ain't gonna lie, I ain't gonna lie,
   'Cause I'm tired of the fake love. Show me what you're made of. Boy, make me believe.
   Whoa, hold up, girl. Don't you know you're beautiful? And it's easy to see.

Perfect

Words and Music by Ed Sheeran

*Capo I

Strum Pattern: 8
Pick Pattern: 9

Intro
Slow, in 4

Verse

1. I found a love for _____ me. Dar - ling, just

2. *See additional lyrics*

*Optional: To match recording, place capo at 1st fret.

dive _ right in, fol - low my lead. Well, I found a girl, beau - ti -

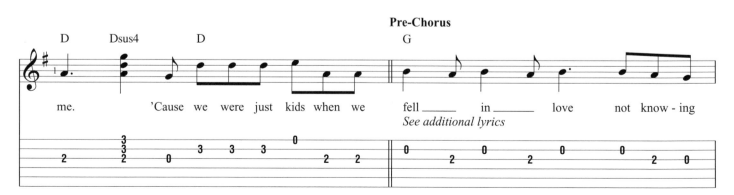

ful and sweet. Well, I nev - er knew you were _ the some - one wait - ing for

Pre-Chorus

me. 'Cause we were just kids when we fell _____ in _____ love not know - ing

See additional lyrics

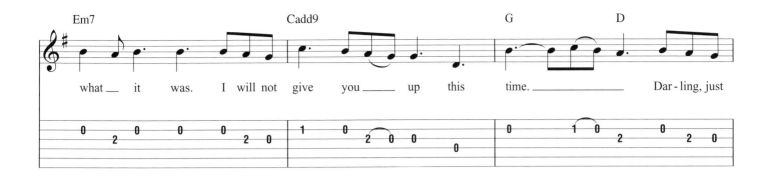

what __ it was. I will not give you ____ up this time. _____ Dar - ling, just

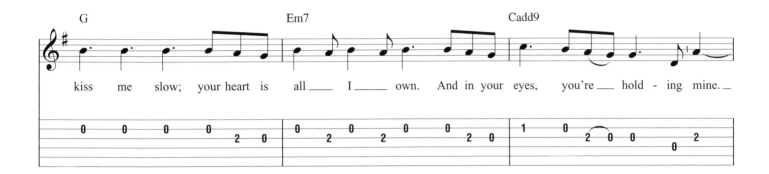

kiss me slow; your heart is all ___ I _____ own. And in your eyes, you're __ hold - ing mine. __

Chorus

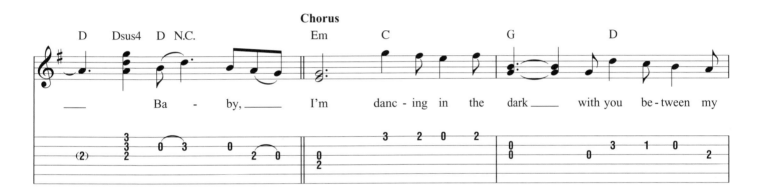

___ Ba - by, _____ I'm danc - ing in the dark ____ with you be - tween my

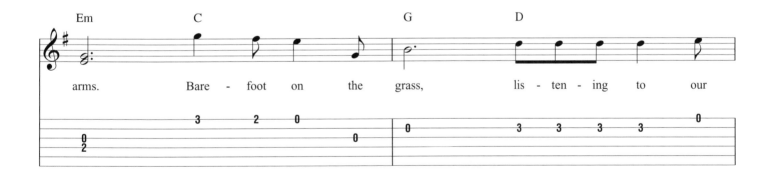

arms. Bare - foot on the grass, lis - ten - ing to our

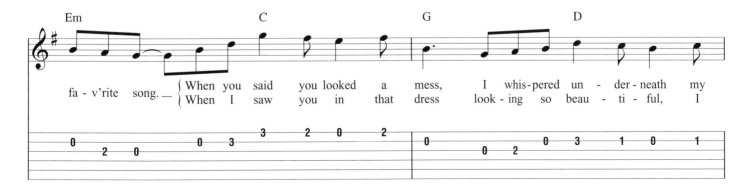

fa - v'rite song. — { When you said you looked a mess, I whis - pered un - der - neath my
{ When I saw you in that dress look - ing so beau - ti - ful, I

breath, but you heard it. Dar - ling, you look per - fect to -
don't de - serve this. Dar - ling,

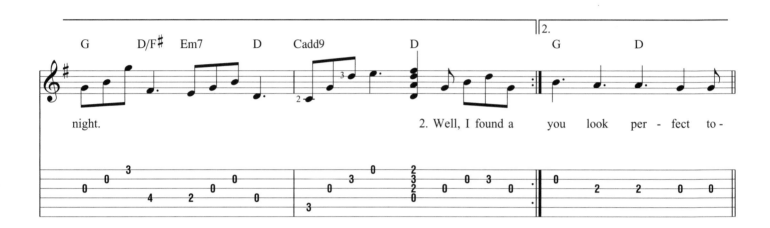

night.

2. Well, I found a   you   look   per - fect to -

Interlude

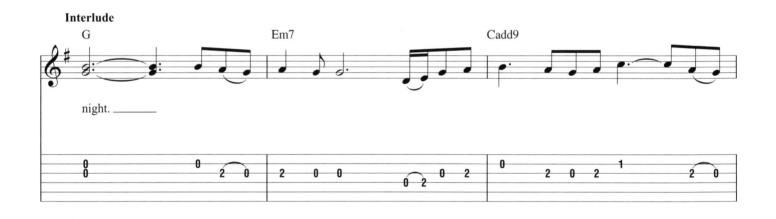

night. _____

Outro-Chorus

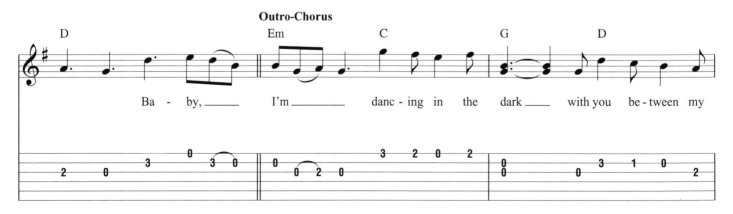

Ba - by, _____ I'm _____ danc - ing in the dark ___ with you be - tween my

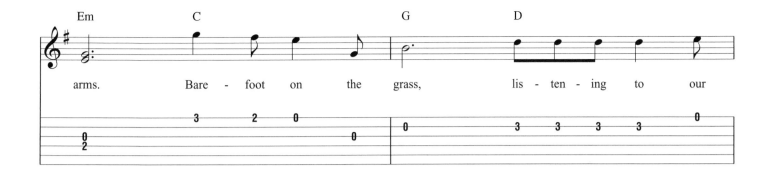

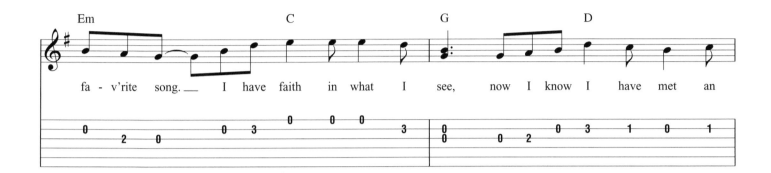

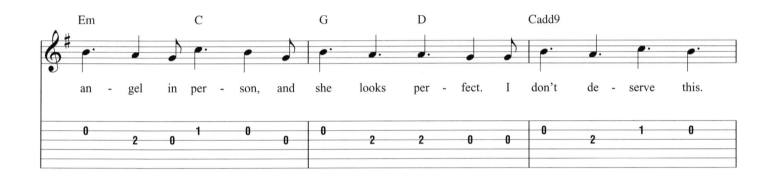

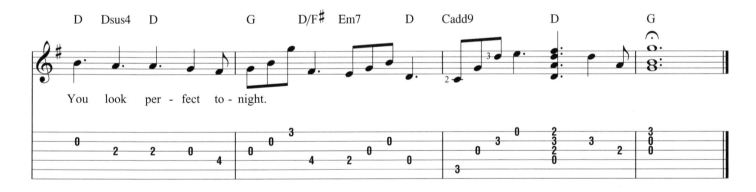

Additional Lyrics

2. Well, I found a woman, stronger than anyone I know.
   She shares my dreams, I hope that someday, I'll share her home.
   I found a love to carry more than just my secrets,
   To carry love, to carry children of our own.

Pre-Chorus We are still kids, but we're so in love, fighting against all odds.
   I know we'll be all right this time.
   Darling, just hold my hand; be my girl, I'll be your man.
   I've seen the future in your eyes.

Praying

Words and Music by Kesha Sebert, Ben Abraham, Ryan Lewis and Andrew Joslyn

Pre-Chorus

you brought the flames and you put me through hell. I had to learn how to fight for my-self.

And we both know all the truth I could tell. I'll just say this is, "I wish you fare - well."

Chorus

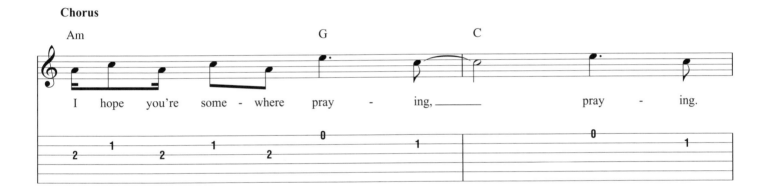

I hope you're some - where pray - ing, pray - ing.

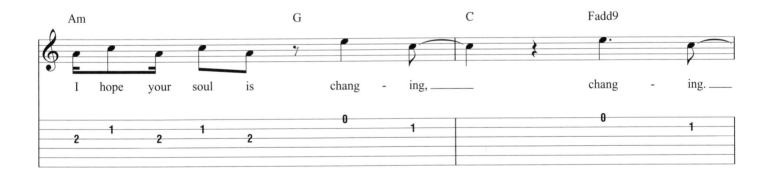

I hope your soul is chang - ing, chang - ing.

I hope you find your peace fall - ing on your

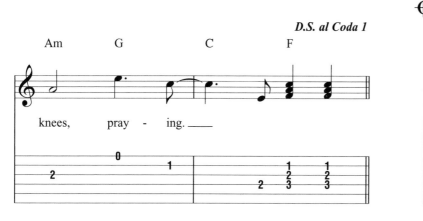

*Sung one octave higher, till end.

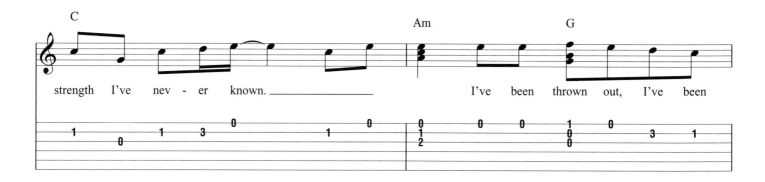

Pre-Chorus

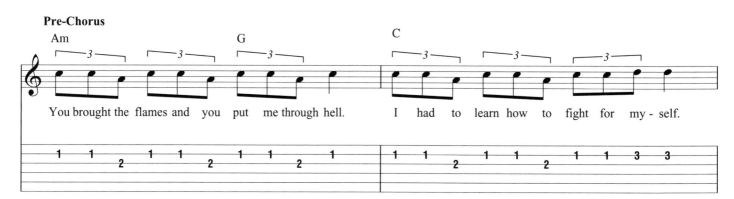

And we both know all the truth I could tell. __ I'll just say this is, "I wish you fare - well." __

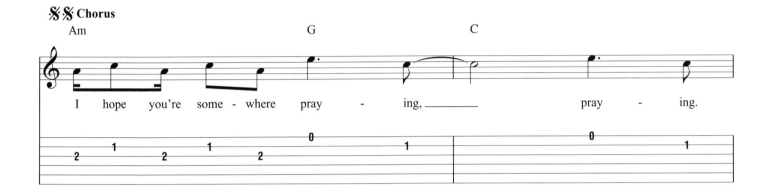

𝄋 𝄋 Chorus

I hope you're some - where pray - ing, ___ pray - ing.

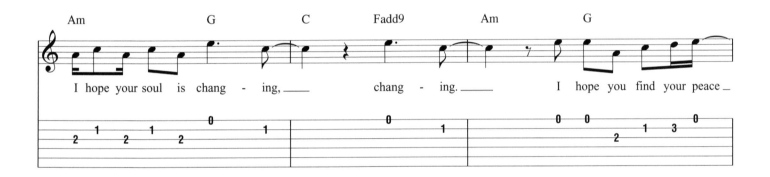

I hope your soul is chang - ing, ___ chang - ing. ___ I hope you find your peace __

To Coda 2 ⊕

__ fall - ing on __ your knees, pray - ing. ___ Oh, some -

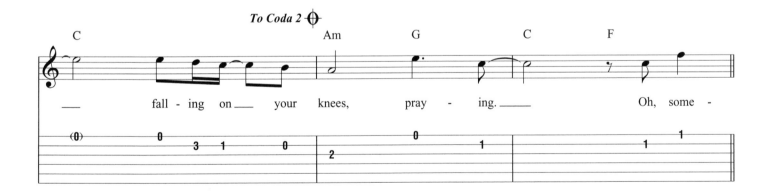

Bridge

times I pray for you at night, ___ oh. Some -

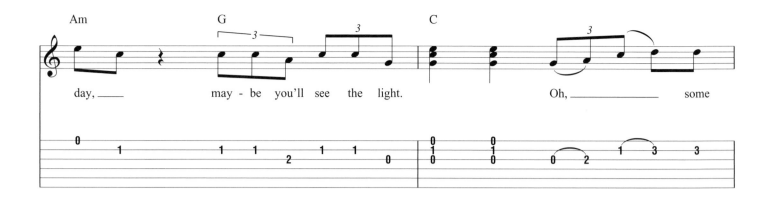

day, _____ may - be you'll see the light. Oh, _____ some

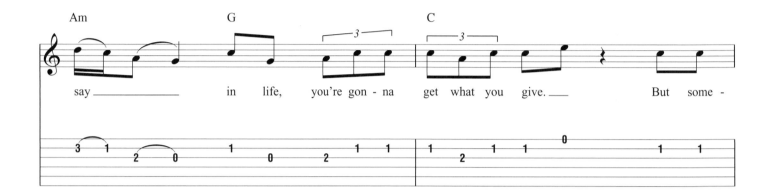

say _____ in life, you're gon - na get what you give. _____ But some -

D.S.S. al Coda 2

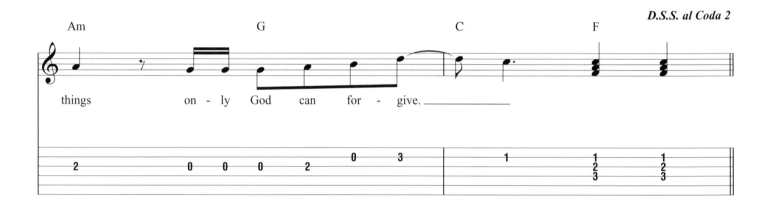

things on - ly God can for - give. _____

⊕ Coda 2

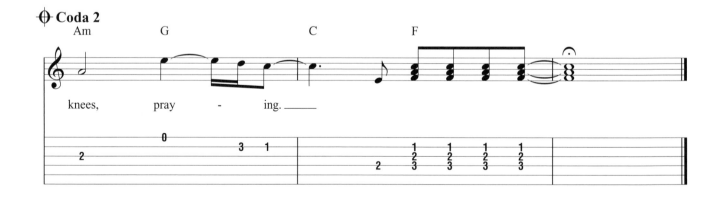

knees, pray - ing. _____

Additional Lyrics

2. I'm proud of who I am.
   No more monsters; I can breathe again.
   And you said that I was done.
   Well, you were wrong
   And now the best is yet to come.

...Ready for It?

Words and Music by Taylor Swift, Max Martin, Shellback and Ali Payami

*Capo VII

Strum Pattern: 3
Pick Pattern: 3

Intro
Moderately slow, in 2

*Optional: To match recording, place capo at 7th fret.

Verse

1. Knew he was a kil- ler first time that I saw him. Won- der how man-
   rob- ber first time that he saw me, steal- in' hearts and

y girls he had loved and left haunt- ed. But if he's a ghost, then I can be a
run- nin' off and nev- er say- in' sor- ry. But if I'm a thief, then he can join the

phan- tom, hold- ing him for ran- som. Some,_____ some boys are try- in'
heist and we'll move to an is- land. And,_____ and he can be my

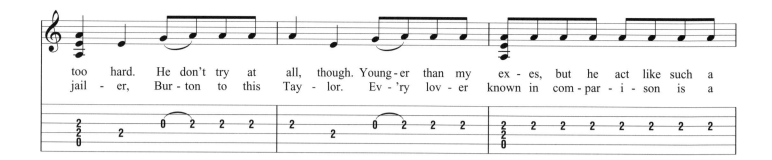

too hard. He don't try at all, though. Young-er than my ex-es, but he act like such a
jail-er, Bur-ton to this Tay-lor. Ev-'ry lov-er known in com-par-i-son is a

man, so I see noth-ing bet-ter. I keep him for-ev-er like a ven-
fail-ure. I for-get their names now. I'm so ver-y tame now. Nev-er be the

Pre-Chorus

A5

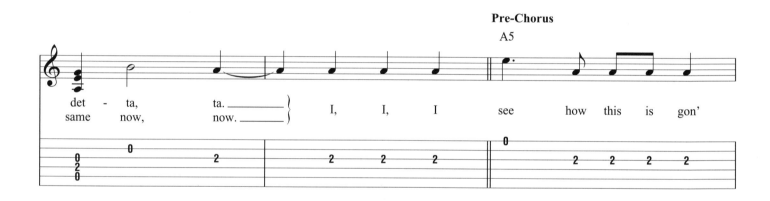

det-ta, ta. ⎫ I, I, I, I see how this is gon'
same now, now. ⎭

go. Touch me and you'll nev-er be a-lone. I, is-land

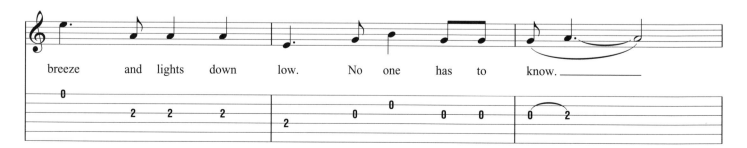

breeze and lights down low. No one has to know.

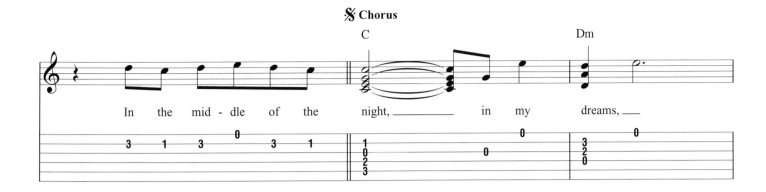

In the mid - dle of the night, _____ in my dreams, _____

you should see the things we do, ba -

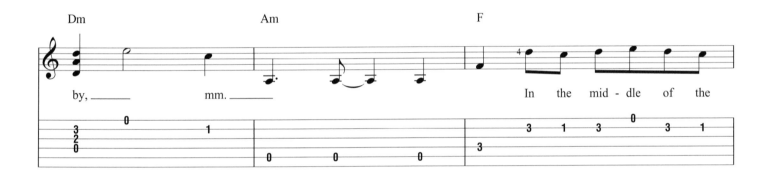

by, _____ mm. _____ In the mid - dle of the

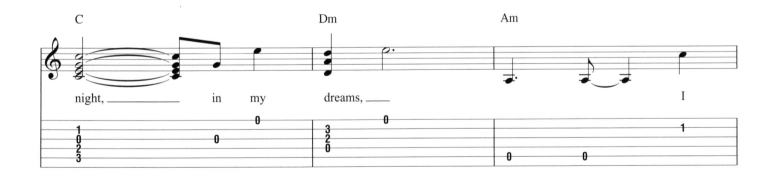

night, _____ in my dreams, _____ I

3rd time, To Coda

know I'm gon - na be with you, so I'll take my time. _____

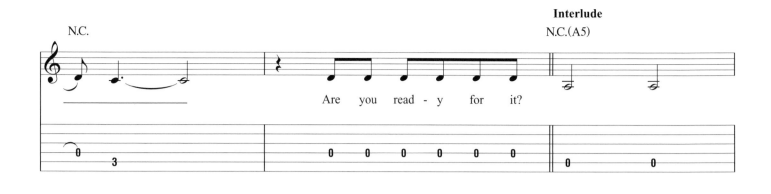

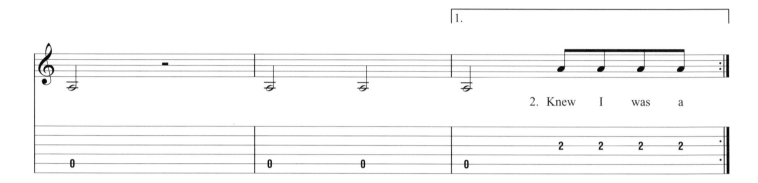

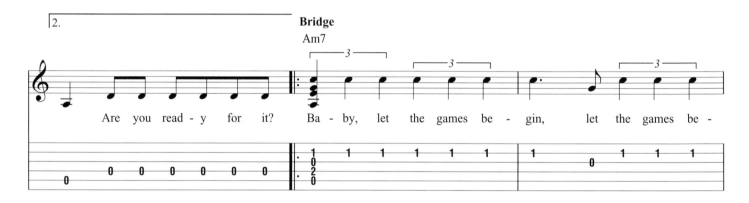

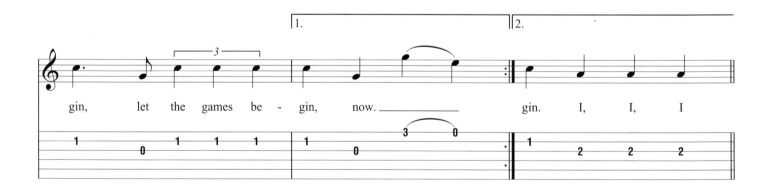

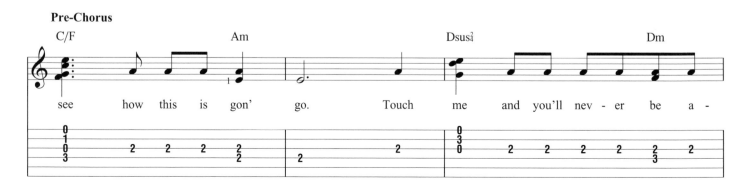

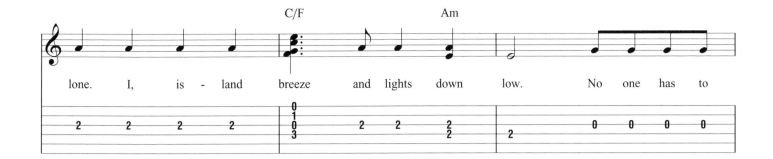

lone.   I,   is - land   breeze   and   lights   down   low.   No   one   has   to

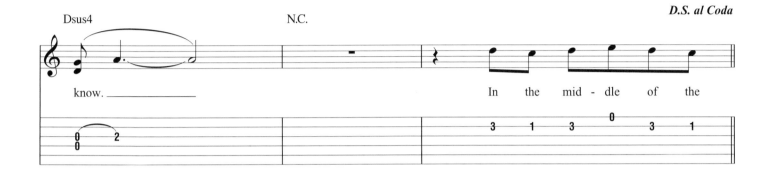

D.S. al Coda

know. _____

In   the   mid - dle   of   the

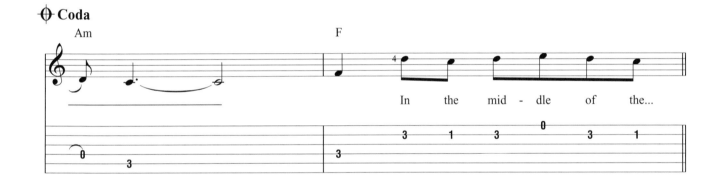

Coda

In   the   mid - dle   of   the...

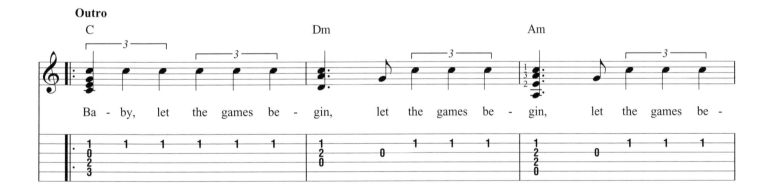

Outro

Ba - by,   let   the   games   be - gin,   let   the   games   be - gin,   let   the   games   be -

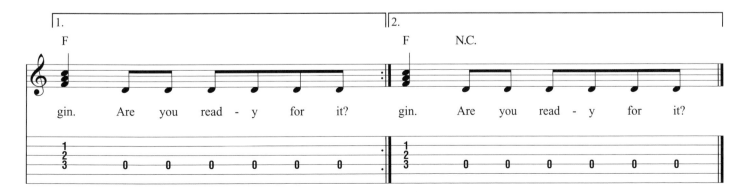

gin.   Are   you   read - y   for   it?   gin.   Are   you   read - y   for   it?

Say Something

Words and Music by Justin Timberlake, Chris Stapleton, Nate Hills, Larrance Dopson and Tim Mosley

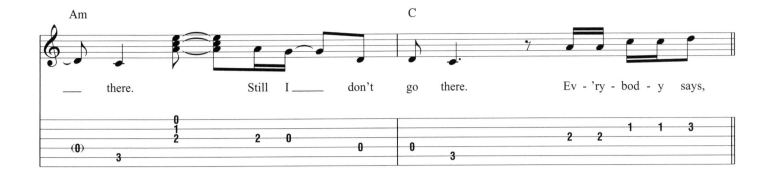

𝄋 Chorus

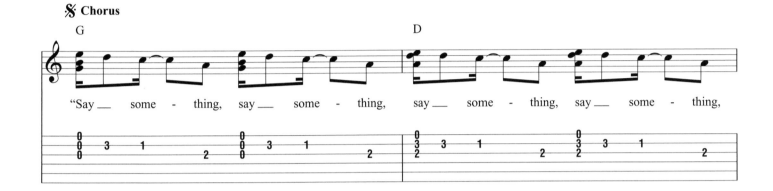

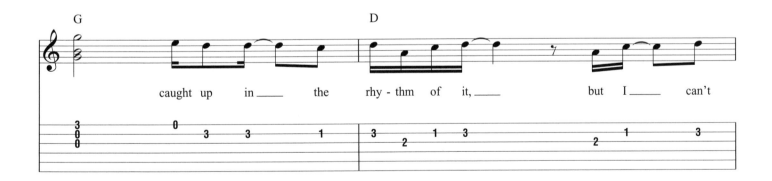

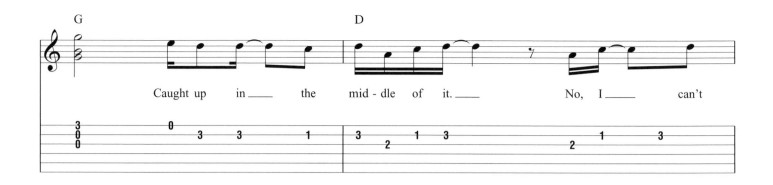

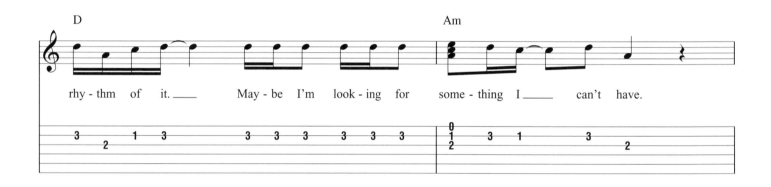

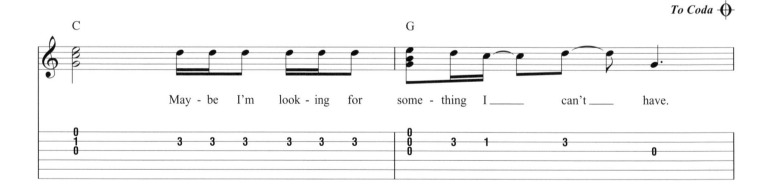

Verse

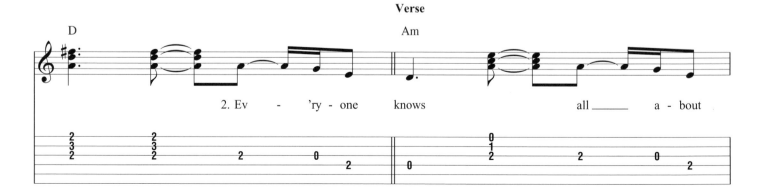

*Chord symbols in parentheses
reflect implied harmony.

Some-times the great-est way to say __ some-thing is to say noth-ing at __ all.

Bridge

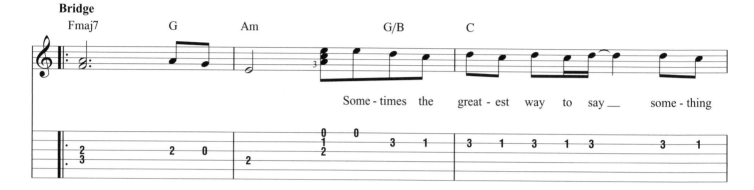

Some-times the great-est way to say __ some-thing

is to say noth-ing at __ all. is to say noth-ing. But I can't

Chorus

help my-self. __ No, I __ can't help my-self, __ no, no. Caught up in __ the

mid-dle of it. __ No, I __ can't help my-self. __ No, I __ can't help my-self, __ no, no,

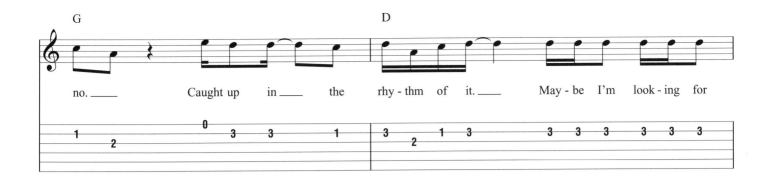

no. ____ Caught up in ____ the rhy - thm of it. ____ May - be I'm look - ing for

some - thing I ____ can't have. May - be I'm look - ing for some - thing I ____ can't _ have.

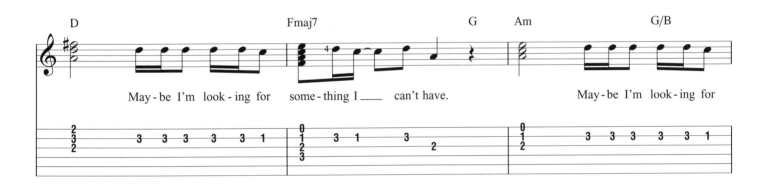

May - be I'm look - ing for some - thing I ____ can't have. May - be I'm look - ing for

Outro

some - thing I ____ can't _ have. Some - times the

great - est way to say ____ some - thing is to say noth - ing at ____ all. is to say noth - ing.

Second One to Know

Words and Music by Chris Stapleton and Mike Henderson

*Optional: To match recording, place capo at 3rd fret.

Don't put my love on your back burn-er.

Nev-er let an-y-thing__ that hot get cold. And

if you ev-er change your mind,__ wan-na leave my love__ be-hind,__ just

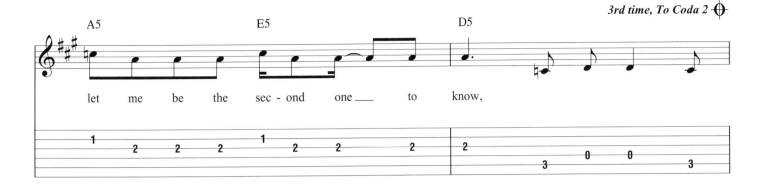

let me be the sec - ond one ___ to know,

To Coda 1

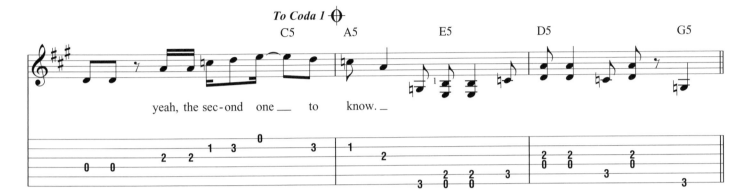

yeah, the sec-ond one ___ to know. ___

Verse

1. Hold up my right hand, swear there's a prom - ised land. ___

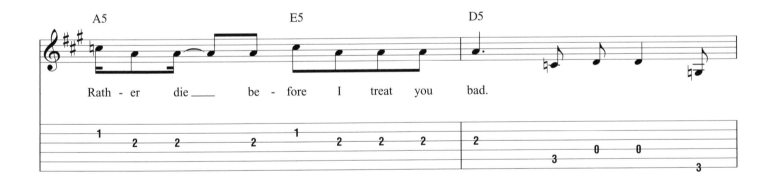

Rath - er die ___ be - fore I treat you bad.

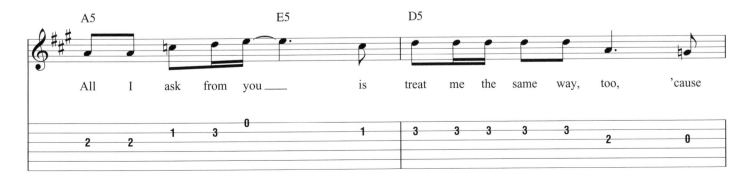

All I ask from you ___ is treat me the same way, too, 'cause

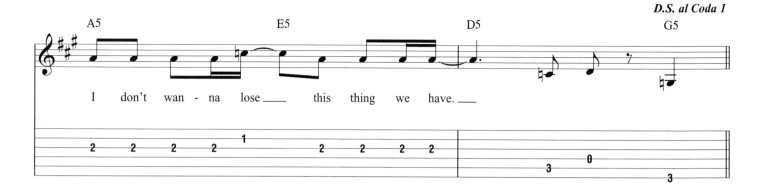

I don't wan - na lose ____ this thing we have. ____

⊕ Coda 1

Interlude **Guitar Solo**

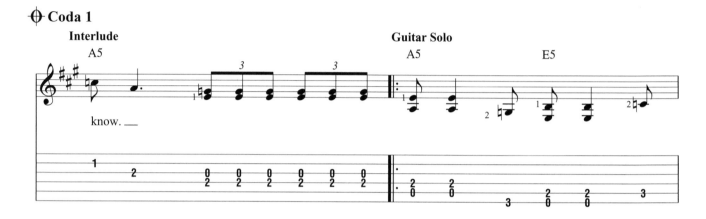

know. ____

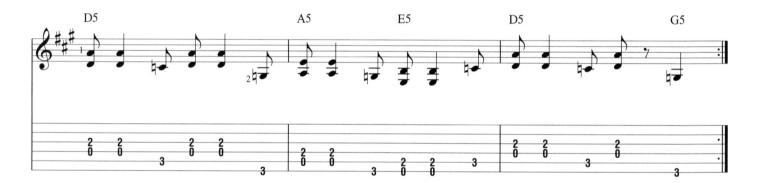

Verse

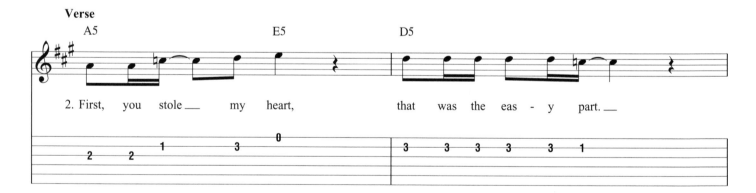

2. First, you stole ____ my heart, that was the eas - y part. ____

Don't ev - er tell me that crime ___ don't pay.

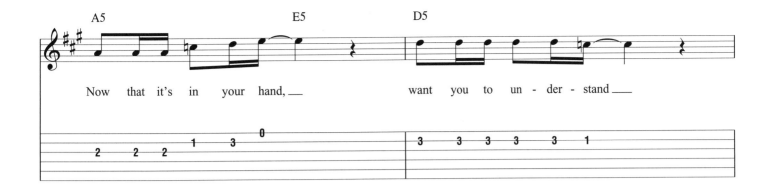

Now that it's in your hand, ___ want you to un - der - stand ___

D.S. al Coda 2

I would-'ve giv - en it to you an - y - way. ___

Coda 2

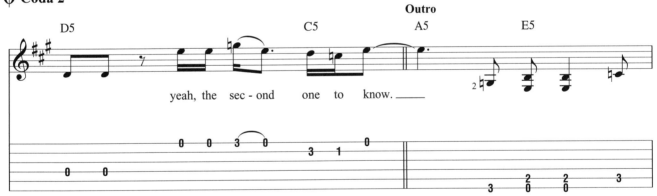

Outro

yeah, the sec - ond one to know. ___

Repeat and fade

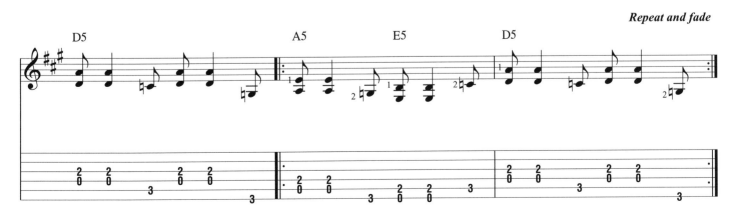

Sweet Creature

Words and Music by Harry Styles and Thomas Hull

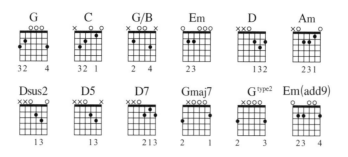

Strum Pattern: 2, 4
Pick Pattern: 4, 6

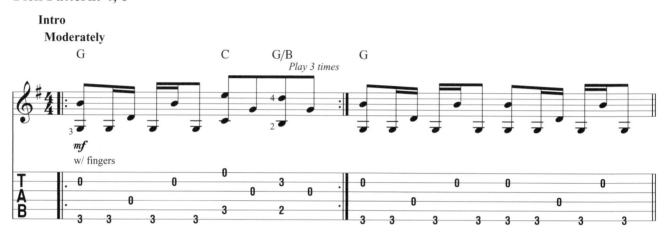

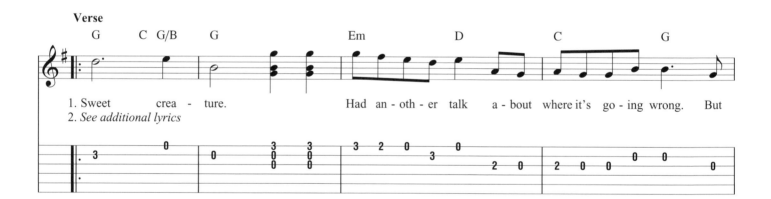

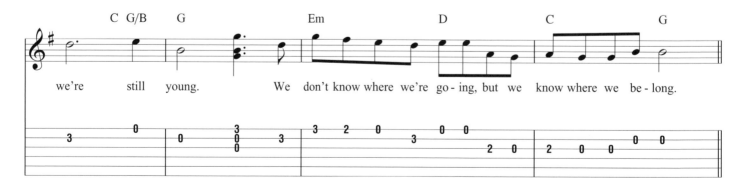

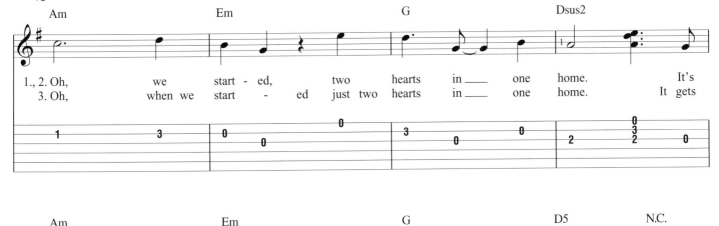

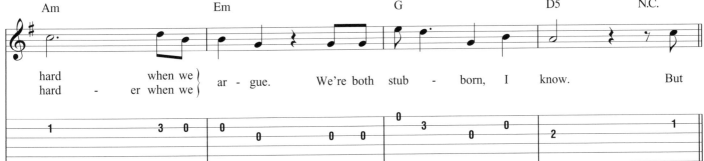

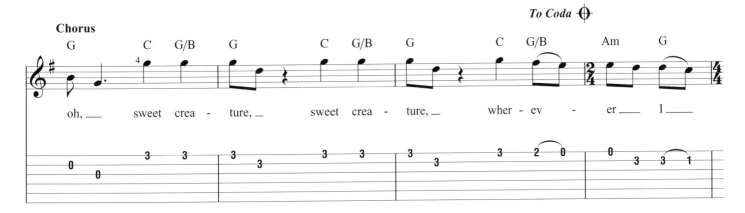

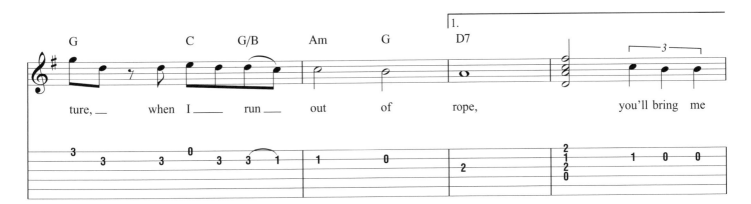

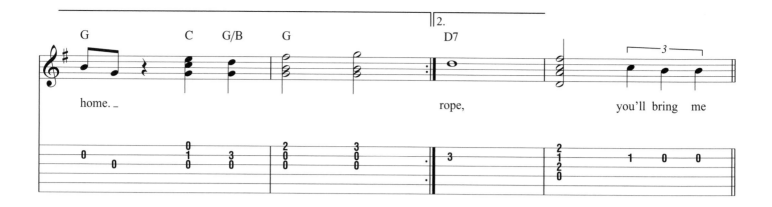

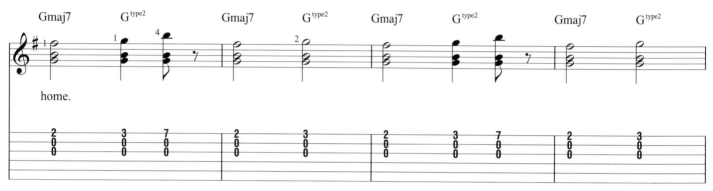

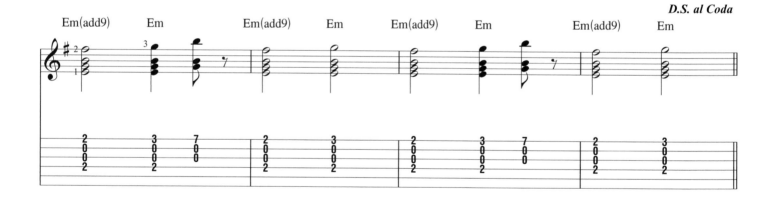

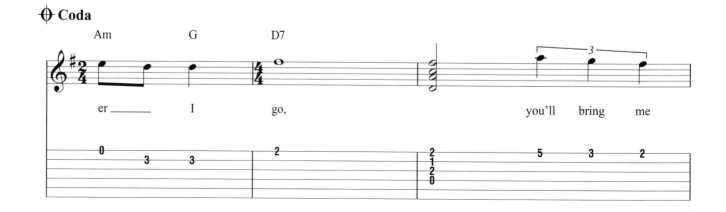

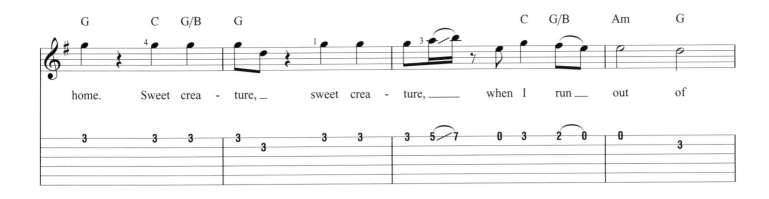

home. Sweet crea - ture,_ sweet crea - ture,____ when I run_ out of

rope,_____ you'll bring me home.

You'll bring me

Outro

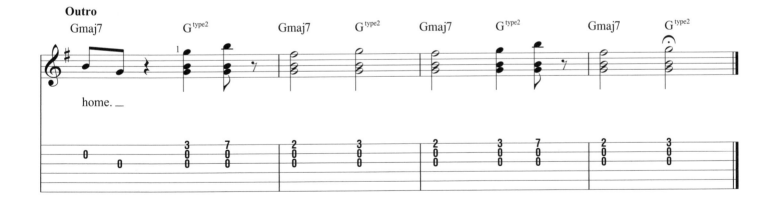

home._

Additional Lyrics

2. Sweet creature.
   Runnin' through the garden, oh, where nothin' bothered us.
   But we're still young.
   Always think about you and how we don't speak enough.

Thunder

**Words and Music by Dan Reynolds, Wayne Sermon, Ben McKee,
Daniel Platzman, Alexander Grant and Jayson DeZuzio**

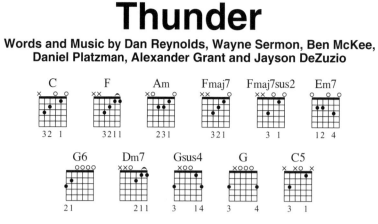

Strum Pattern: 1, 3
Pick Pattern: 2, 5

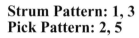

Verse
Moderately slow

1. Just a young gun with a quick fuse, I was up - tight, want to let loose.

I was dream - ing of big - ger things and want to leave my own life be - hind.

Not a yes sir, not a fol - low - er. Fit the box, fit the mold, have a seat in the

foy - er,   take a num - ber.   I was light - ning   be - fore the thun - der, thun - der.

𝄋 **Chorus**

Thun - der,   thun - der, thun,   thun - der,   thu - thu - thun - der, thun - der.

Thun - der,   thun - der, thun,   thun - der,   thu - thu - thun - der, thun - der.

Thun - der, ___   feel the thun - der, ___   light - ning and the thun - der. ___

To Coda

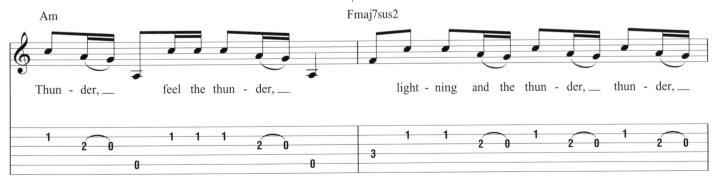

Thun - der, ___   feel the thun - der, ___   light - ning and the thun - der, ___ thun - der, ___

Verse

2. Kids were laugh - ing   in   my class - es   while   I   was schem - ing   for   the mass - es.

"Who   do   you   think   you   are   dream - ing 'bout   be - ing   a   big   star?"

You say you're bas - ic,   you say you're eas - y,   you're al - ways rid - ing   in   the back   seat.

D.S. al Coda

Now I'm smil - ing   from the stage   while   you were clap - ping   in   the nose - bleeds.

⊕ Coda

light - ning and the thun - der, _____ thun - der. _____

Interlude

Chorus

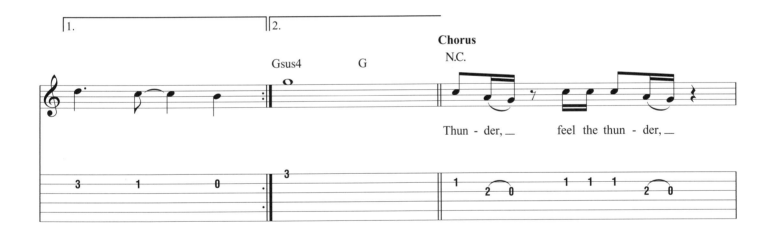

Thun - der, _ feel the thun - der, _

light - ning and the thun - der, _ thun - der. _ Thun - der, _ feel the thun - der, _

light - ning   and the thun - der, __ thun - der. __   Thun - der, __   feel the thun - der, __

1.

Fmaj7sus2

light - ning   and the thun - der, __ thun - der. __

2.

Fmaj7sus2

light - ning   and the thun - der, __ thun - der. __

Outro

C

Am   F   C5

Too Good at Goodbyes

Words and Music by Sam Smith, Tor Hermansen, Mikkel Eriksen and James Napier

*Capo V

Strum Pattern: 3
Pick Pattern: 3

*Optional: To match recording, place capo at 5th fret.

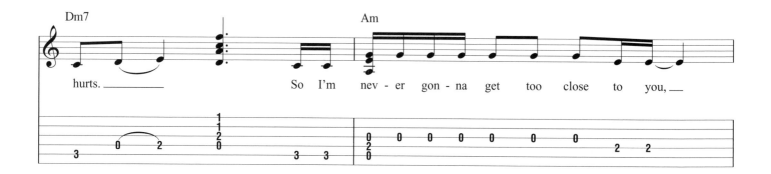

hurts. _____ So I'm nev - er gon - na get too close to you, ___

e - ven when I mean the most to you, ___ in case you go and leave me in the

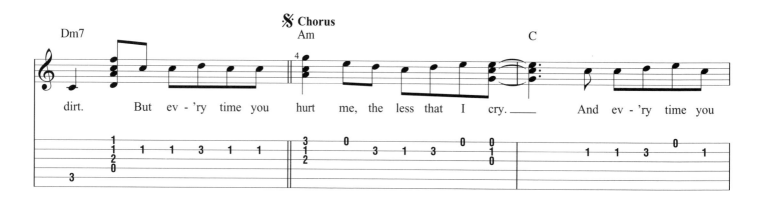

𝄋 Chorus

dirt. But ev - 'ry time you hurt me, the less that I cry. ___ And ev - 'ry time you

leave me, the quick - er these tears ___ dry. And ev - 'ry time you walk out, the less I love you.

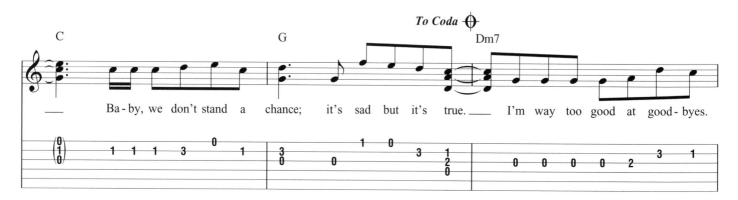

To Coda ⊕

_ Ba - by, we don't stand a chance; it's sad but it's true. ___ I'm way too good at good - byes.

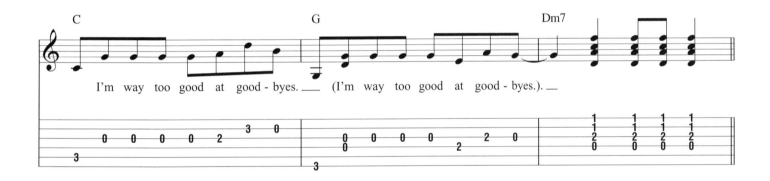

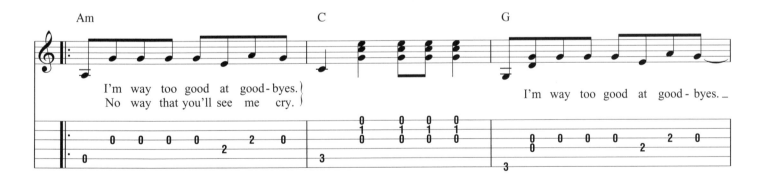

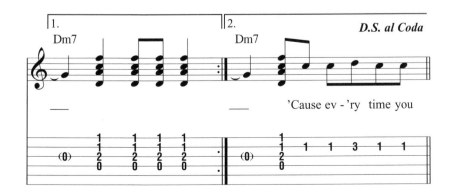

EASY GUITAR WITH NOTES & TAB

This series features simplified arrangements with notes, tab, chord charts, and strum and pick patterns.

MIXED FOLIOS

00702287	Acoustic	$14.99
00702002	Acoustic Rock Hits for Easy Guitar	$14.99
00702166	All-Time Best Guitar Collection	$19.99
00699665	Beatles Best	$14.99
00702232	Best Acoustic Songs for Easy Guitar	$14.99
00119835	Best Children's Songs	$16.99
00702233	Best Hard Rock Songs	$14.99
00703055	The Big Book of Nursery Rhymes & Children's Songs	$14.99
00322179	The Big Easy Book of Classic Rock Guitar	$24.95
00698978	Big Christmas Collection	$16.95
00702394	Bluegrass Songs for Easy Guitar	$12.99
00703387	Celtic Classics	$14.99
00224808	Chart Hits of 2016-2017	$14.99
00702149	Children's Christian Songbook	$9.99
00702237	Christian Acoustic Favorites	$12.95
00702028	Christmas Classics	$8.99
00101779	Christmas Guitar	$14.99
00702185	Christmas Hits	$9.95
00702141	Classic Rock	$8.95
00702203	CMT's 100 Greatest Country Songs	$27.95
00702283	The Contemporary Christian Collection	$16.99
00702239	Country Classics for Easy Guitar	$19.99
00702282	Country Hits of 2009–2010	$14.99
00702257	Easy Acoustic Guitar Songs	$14.99
00702280	Easy Guitar Tab White Pages	$29.99
00702041	Favorite Hymns for Easy Guitar	$10.99
00140841	4-Chord Hymns for Guitar	$7.99
00702281	4 Chord Rock	$10.99
00126894	Frozen	$14.99
00702286	Glee	$16.99
00699374	Gospel Favorites	$14.95
00122138	The Grammy Awards® Record of the Year 1958-2011	$19.99
00702160	The Great American Country Songbook	$16.99
00702050	Great Classical Themes for Easy Guitar	$8.99
00702116	Greatest Hymns for Guitar	$10.99
00702130	The Groovy Years	$9.95
00702184	Guitar Instrumentals	$9.95
00148030	Halloween Guitar Songs	$14.99
00702273	Irish Songs	$12.99
00702275	Jazz Favorites for Easy Guitar	$15.99
00702274	Jazz Standards for Easy Guitar	$15.99
00702162	Jumbo Easy Guitar Songbook	$19.99
00702258	Legends of Rock	$14.99
00702261	Modern Worship Hits	$14.99
00702189	MTV's 100 Greatest Pop Songs	$24.95
00702272	1950s Rock	$15.99
00702271	1960s Rock	$15.99
00702270	1970s Rock	$15.99
00702269	1980s Rock	$14.99
00702268	1990s Rock	$14.99
00109725	Once	$14.99
00702187	Selections from O Brother Where Art Thou?	$14.99
00702178	100 Songs for Kids	$14.99
00702515	Pirates of the Caribbean	$12.99
00702125	Praise and Worship for Guitar	$10.99
00702285	Southern Rock Hits	$12.99
00121535	30 Easy Celtic Guitar Solos	$14.99
00702220	Today's Country Hits	$9.95
00121900	Today's Women of Pop & Rock	$14.99
00702294	Top Worship Hits	$15.99
00702255	VH1's 100 Greatest Hard Rock Songs	$27.95
00702175	VH1's 100 Greatest Songs of Rock and Roll	$24.95
00702253	Wicked	$12.99

ARTIST COLLECTIONS

00702267	AC/DC for Easy Guitar	$15.99
00702598	Adele for Easy Guitar	$15.99
00702040	Best of the Allman Brothers	$14.99
00702865	J.S. Bach for Easy Guitar	$14.99
00702169	Best of The Beach Boys	$12.99
00702292	The Beatles — 1	$19.99
00125796	Best of Chuck Berry	$14.99
00702201	The Essential Black Sabbath	$12.95
02501615	Zac Brown Band — The Foundation	$16.99
02501621	Zac Brown Band — You Get What You Give	$16.99
00702043	Best of Johnny Cash	$16.99
00702263	Best of Casting Crowns	$14.99
00702090	Eric Clapton's Best	$10.95
00702086	Eric Clapton — from the Album Unplugged	$10.95
00702202	The Essential Eric Clapton	$14.99
00702250	blink-182 — Greatest Hits	$15.99
00702053	Best of Patsy Cline	$12.99
00702229	The Very Best of Creedence Clearwater Revival	$15.99
00702145	Best of Jim Croce	$15.99
00702278	Crosby, Stills & Nash	$12.99
00702219	David Crowder*Band Collection	$12.95
14042809	Bob Dylan	$14.99
00702276	Fleetwood Mac — Easy Guitar Collection	$14.99
00130952	Foo Fighters	$14.99
00139462	The Very Best of Grateful Dead	$14.99
00702136	Best of Merle Haggard	$12.99
00702227	Jimi Hendrix — Smash Hits	$14.99
00702288	Best of Hillsong United	$12.99
00702236	Best of Antonio Carlos Jobim	$14.99
00702245	Elton John — Greatest Hits 1970–2002	$14.99
00129855	Jack Johnson	$14.99
00702204	Robert Johnson	$10.99
00702234	Selections from Toby Keith — 35 Biggest Hits	$12.95
00702003	Kiss	$10.99
00110578	Best of Kutless	$12.99
00702216	Lynyrd Skynyrd	$15.99
00702182	The Essential Bob Marley	$12.95
00146081	Maroon 5	$14.99
00121925	Bruno Mars – Unorthodox Jukebox	$12.99
00702248	Paul McCartney — All the Best	$14.99
00702129	Songs of Sarah McLachlan	$12.95
00125484	The Best of MercyMe	$12.99
02501316	Metallica — Death Magnetic	$17.99
00702209	Steve Miller Band — Young Hearts (Greatest Hits)	$12.95
00124167	Jason Mraz	$15.99
00702096	Best of Nirvana	$15.99
00702211	The Offspring — Greatest Hits	$12.95
00138026	One Direction	$14.99
00702030	Best of Roy Orbison	$14.99
00702144	Best of Ozzy Osbourne	$14.99
00702279	Tom Petty	$12.99
00102911	Pink Floyd	$16.99
00702139	Elvis Country Favorites	$12.99
00702293	The Very Best of Prince	$14.99
00699415	Best of Queen for Guitar	$14.99
00109279	Best of R.E.M.	$14.99
00702208	Red Hot Chili Peppers — Greatest Hits	$12.95
00174793	The Very Best of Santana	$14.99
00702196	Best of Bob Seger	$12.95
00146046	Ed Sheeran	$14.99
00702252	Frank Sinatra — Nothing But the Best	$12.99
00702010	Best of Rod Stewart	$16.99
00702049	Best of George Strait	$14.99
00702259	Taylor Swift for Easy Guitar	$15.99
00702260	Taylor Swift — Fearless	$14.99
00139727	Taylor Swift — 1989	$17.99
00115960	Taylor Swift — Red	$16.99
00253667	Taylor Swift — Reputation	$17.99
00702290	Taylor Swift — Speak Now	$15.99
00702226	Chris Tomlin — See the Morning	$12.95
00148643	Train	$14.99
00702427	U2 — 18 Singles	$14.99
00102711	Van Halen	$16.99
00702108	Best of Stevie Ray Vaughan	$14.99
00702123	Best of Hank Williams	$14.99
00702111	Stevie Wonder — Guitar Collection	$9.95
00702228	Neil Young — Greatest Hits	$15.99
00119133	Neil Young — Harvest	$14.99
00702188	Essential ZZ Top	$10.95

Prices, contents and availability subject to change without notice.

HAL·LEONARD GUITAR PLAY-ALONG

AUDIO ACCESS INCLUDED

This series will help you play your favorite songs quickly and easily. Just follow the tab and listen to the audio to the hear how the guitar should sound, and then play along using the separate backing tracks. Audio files also include software to slow down the tempo without changing pitch. The melody and lyrics are included in the book so that you can sing or simply follow along.

INCLUDES TAB

VOL. 1 – ROCK	00699570 / $16.99
VOL. 2 – ACOUSTIC	00699569 / $16.99
VOL. 3 – HARD ROCK	00699573 / $17.99
VOL. 4 – POP/ROCK	00699571 / $16.99
VOL. 6 – '90S ROCK	00699572 / $16.99
VOL. 7 – BLUES	00699575 / $17.99
VOL. 8 – ROCK	00699585 / $16.99
VOL. 9 – EASY ACOUSTIC SONGS	00151708 / $16.99
VOL. 10 – ACOUSTIC	00699586 / $16.95
VOL. 11 – EARLY ROCK	00699579 / $14.95
VOL. 12 – POP/ROCK	00699587 / $14.95
VOL. 13 – FOLK ROCK	00699581 / $16.99
VOL. 14 – BLUES ROCK	00699582 / $16.99
VOL. 15 – R&B	00699583 / $16.99
VOL. 16 – JAZZ	00699584 / $15.95
VOL. 17 – COUNTRY	00699588 / $16.99
VOL. 18 – ACOUSTIC ROCK	00699577 / $15.95
VOL. 19 – SOUL	00699578 / $15.99
VOL. 20 – ROCKABILLY	00699580 / $16.99
VOL. 21 – SANTANA	00174525 / $17.99
VOL. 22 – CHRISTMAS	00699600 / $15.99
VOL. 23 – SURF	00699635 / $15.99
VOL. 24 – ERIC CLAPTON	00699649 / $17.99
VOL. 25 – THE BEATLES	00198265 / $17.99
VOL. 26 – ELVIS PRESLEY	00699643 / $16.99
VOL. 27 – DAVID LEE ROTH	00699645 / $16.95
VOL. 28 – GREG KOCH	00699646 / $16.99
VOL. 29 – BOB SEGER	00699647 / $15.99
VOL. 30 – KISS	00699644 / $16.99
VOL. 31 – CHRISTMAS HITS	00699652 / $14.95
VOL. 32 – THE OFFSPRING	00699653 / $14.95
VOL. 33 – ACOUSTIC CLASSICS	00699656 / $17.99
VOL. 34 – CLASSIC ROCK	00699658 / $17.99
VOL. 35 – HAIR METAL	00699660 / $17.99
VOL. 36 – SOUTHERN ROCK	00699661 / $16.95
VOL. 37 – ACOUSTIC UNPLUGGED	00699662 / $22.99
VOL. 38 – BLUES	00699663 / $16.95
VOL. 39 – '80S METAL	00699664 / $16.99
VOL. 40 – INCUBUS	00699668 / $17.95
VOL. 41 – ERIC CLAPTON	00699669 / $17.99
VOL. 42 – COVER BAND HITS	00211597 / $16.99
VOL. 43 – LYNYRD SKYNYRD	00699681 / $17.95
VOL. 44 – JAZZ	00699689 / $16.99
VOL. 45 – TV THEMES	00699718 / $14.95
VOL. 46 – MAINSTREAM ROCK	00699722 / $16.95
VOL. 47 – HENDRIX SMASH HITS	00699723 / $19.99
VOL. 48 – AEROSMITH CLASSICS	00699724 / $17.99
VOL. 49 – STEVIE RAY VAUGHAN	00699725 / $17.99
VOL. 50 – VAN HALEN 1978-1984	00110269 / $17.99
VOL. 51 – ALTERNATIVE '90S	00699727 / $14.99
VOL. 52 – FUNK	00699728 / $15.99
VOL. 53 – DISCO	00699729 / $14.99
VOL. 54 – HEAVY METAL	00699730 / $15.99
VOL. 55 – POP METAL	00699731 / $14.95
VOL. 56 – FOO FIGHTERS	00699749 / $15.99
VOL. 59 – CHET ATKINS	00702347 / $16.99
VOL. 62 – CHRISTMAS CAROLS	00699798 / $12.95
VOL. 63 – CREEDENCE CLEARWATER REVIVAL	00699802 / $16.99
VOL. 64 – THE ULTIMATE OZZY OSBOURNE	00699803 / $17.99
VOL. 66 – THE ROLLING STONES	00699807 / $17.99
VOL. 67 – BLACK SABBATH	00699808 / $16.99

VOL. 68 – PINK FLOYD – DARK SIDE OF THE MOON	00699809 / $16.99
VOL. 69 – ACOUSTIC FAVORITES	00699810 / $16.99
VOL. 70 – OZZY OSBOURNE	00699805 / $16.99
VOL. 73 – BLUESY ROCK	00699829 / $16.99
VOL. 74 – SIMPLE STRUMMING SONGS	00151706 / $19.99
VOL. 75 – TOM PETTY	00699882 / $16.99
VOL. 76 – COUNTRY HITS	00699884 / $14.95
VOL. 77 – BLUEGRASS	00699910 / $15.99
VOL. 78 – NIRVANA	00700132 / $16.99
VOL. 79 – NEIL YOUNG	00700133 / $24.99
VOL. 80 – ACOUSTIC ANTHOLOGY	00700175 / $19.95
VOL. 81 – ROCK ANTHOLOGY	00700176 / $22.99
VOL. 82 – EASY SONGS	00700177 / $14.99
VOL. 83 – THREE CHORD SONGS	00700178 / $16.99
VOL. 84 – STEELY DAN	00700200 / $16.99
VOL. 85 – THE POLICE	00700269 / $16.99
VOL. 86 – BOSTON	00700465 / $16.99
VOL. 87 – ACOUSTIC WOMEN	00700763 / $14.99
VOL. 89 – REGGAE	00700468 / $15.99
VOL. 90 – CLASSICAL POP	00700469 / $14.99
VOL. 91 – BLUES INSTRUMENTALS	00700505 / $15.99
VOL. 92 – EARLY ROCK INSTRUMENTALS	00700506 / $15.99
VOL. 93 – ROCK INSTRUMENTALS	00700507 / $16.99
VOL. 94 – SLOW BLUES	00700508 / $16.99
VOL. 95 – BLUES CLASSICS	00700509 / $15.99
VOL. 96 – BEST COUNTRY HITS	00211615 / $16.99
VOL. 97 – CHRISTMAS CLASSICS	00236542 / $14.99
VOL. 99 – ZZ TOP	00700762 / $16.99
VOL. 100 – B.B. KING	00700466 / $16.99
VOL. 101 – SONGS FOR BEGINNERS	00701917 / $14.99
VOL. 102 – CLASSIC PUNK	00700769 / $14.99
VOL. 103 – SWITCHFOOT	00700773 / $16.99
VOL. 104 – DUANE ALLMAN	00700846 / $16.99
VOL. 105 – LATIN	00700939 / $16.99
VOL. 106 – WEEZER	00700958 / $14.99
VOL. 107 – CREAM	00701069 / $16.99
VOL. 108 – THE WHO	00701053 / $16.99
VOL. 109 – STEVE MILLER	00701054 / $17.99
VOL. 110 – SLIDE GUITAR HITS	00701055 / $16.99
VOL. 111 – JOHN MELLENCAMP	00701056 / $14.99
VOL. 112 – QUEEN	00701052 / $16.99
VOL. 113 – JIM CROCE	00701058 / $16.99
VOL. 114 – BON JOVI	00701060 / $16.99
VOL. 115 – JOHNNY CASH	00701070 / $16.99
VOL. 116 – THE VENTURES	00701124 / $16.99
VOL. 117 – BRAD PAISLEY	00701224 / $16.99
VOL. 118 – ERIC JOHNSON	00701353 / $16.99
VOL. 119 – AC/DC CLASSICS	00701356 / $17.99
VOL. 120 – PROGRESSIVE ROCK	00701457 / $14.99
VOL. 121 – U2	00701508 / $16.99
VOL. 122 – CROSBY, STILLS & NASH	00701610 / $16.99
VOL. 123 – LENNON & McCARTNEY ACOUSTIC	00701614 / $16.99
VOL. 125 – JEFF BECK	00701687 / $16.99
VOL. 126 – BOB MARLEY	00701701 / $16.99
VOL. 127 – 1970S ROCK	00701739 / $16.99
VOL. 128 – 1960S ROCK	00701740 / $14.99
VOL. 129 – MEGADETH	00701741 / $16.99
VOL. 130 – IRON MAIDEN	00701742 / $17.99
VOL. 131 – 1990S ROCK	00701743 / $14.99
VOL. 132 – COUNTRY ROCK	00701757 / $15.99
VOL. 133 – TAYLOR SWIFT	00701894 / $16.99
VOL. 134 – AVENGED SEVENFOLD	00701906 / $16.99

VOL. 135 – MINOR BLUES	00151350 / $17.99
VOL. 136 – GUITAR THEMES	00701922 / $14.99
VOL. 137 – IRISH TUNES	00701966 / $15.99
VOL. 138 – BLUEGRASS CLASSICS	00701967 / $16.99
VOL. 139 – GARY MOORE	00702370 / $16.99
VOL. 140 – MORE STEVIE RAY VAUGHAN	00702396 / $17.99
VOL. 141 – ACOUSTIC HITS	00702401 / $16.99
VOL. 143 – SLASH	00702425 / $19.99
VOL. 144 – DJANGO REINHARDT	00702531 / $16.99
VOL. 145 – DEF LEPPARD	00702532 / $17.99
VOL. 146 – ROBERT JOHNSON	00702533 / $16.99
VOL. 147 – SIMON & GARFUNKEL	14041591 / $16.99
VOL. 148 – BOB DYLAN	14041592 / $16.99
VOL. 149 – AC/DC HITS	14041593 / $17.99
VOL. 150 – ZAKK WYLDE	02501717 / $16.99
VOL. 151 – J.S. BACH	02501730 / $16.99
VOL. 152 – JOE BONAMASSA	02501751 / $19.99
VOL. 153 – RED HOT CHILI PEPPERS	00702990 / $19.99
VOL. 155 – ERIC CLAPTON – FROM THE ALBUM UNPLUGGED	00703085 / $16.99
VOL. 156 – SLAYER	00703770 / $17.99
VOL. 157 – FLEETWOOD MAC	00101382 / $16.99
VOL. 158 – ULTIMATE CHRISTMAS	00101889 / $14.99
VOL. 159 – WES MONTGOMERY	00102593 / $19.99
VOL. 160 – T-BONE WALKER	00102641 / $16.99
VOL. 161 – THE EAGLES – ACOUSTIC	00102659 / $17.99
VOL. 162 – THE EAGLES HITS	00102667 / $17.99
VOL. 163 – PANTERA	00103036 / $17.99
VOL. 164 – VAN HALEN 1986-1995	00110270 / $17.99
VOL. 165 – GREEN DAY	00210343 / $17.99
VOL. 166 – MODERN BLUES	00700764 / $16.99
VOL. 167 – DREAM THEATER	00111938 / $24.99
VOL. 168 – KISS	00113421 / $16.99
VOL. 169 – TAYLOR SWIFT	00115982 / $16.99
VOL. 170 – THREE DAYS GRACE	00117337 / $16.99
VOL. 171 – JAMES BROWN	00117420 / $16.99
VOL. 172 – THE DOOBIE BROTHERS	00119670 / $16.99
VOL. 173 – TRANS-SIBERIAN ORCHESTRA	00119907 / $19.99
VOL. 174 – SCORPIONS	00122119 / $16.99
VOL. 175 – MICHAEL SCHENKER	00122127 / $16.99
VOL. 176 – BLUES BREAKERS WITH JOHN MAYALL & ERIC CLAPTON	00122132 / $19.99
VOL. 177 – ALBERT KING	00123271 / $16.99
VOL. 178 – JASON MRAZ	00124165 / $17.99
VOL. 179 – RAMONES	00127073 / $16.99
VOL. 180 – BRUNO MARS	00129706 / $16.99
VOL. 181 – JACK JOHNSON	00129854 / $16.99
VOL. 182 – SOUNDGARDEN	00138161 / $17.99
VOL. 183 – BUDDY GUY	00138240 / $17.99
VOL. 184 – KENNY WAYNE SHEPHERD	00138258 / $17.99
VOL. 185 – JOE SATRIANI	00139457 / $17.99
VOL. 186 – GRATEFUL DEAD	00139459 / $17.99
VOL. 187 – JOHN DENVER	00140839 / $17.99
VOL. 188 – MÖTLEY CRÜE	00141145 / $17.99
VOL. 189 – JOHN MAYER	00144350 / $17.99
VOL. 191 – PINK FLOYD CLASSICS	00146164 / $17.99
VOL. 192 – JUDAS PRIEST	00151352 / $17.99

Prices, contents, and availability subject to change without notice.

Complete song lists available online.

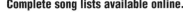

HAL·LEONARD®
www.halleonard.com

0218

DELUXE GUITAR PLAY-ALONG

AUDIO ACCESS INCLUDED 🔊

The Deluxe Guitar Play-Along series will help you play songs faster than ever before! Accurate, easy-to-read guitar tab and professional, customizable audio for 15 songs. The interactive, online audio interface includes tempo/pitch control, looping, buttons to turn instruments on or off, and guitar tab with follow-along marker. The price of each book includes access to audio tracks online using the unique code inside. The tracks can also be downloaded and played offline. Now including PLAYBACK+, a multi-functional audio player that allows you to slow down audio, change pitch, set loop points, and pan left or right – available exclusively from Hal Leonard.

1. TOP ROCK HITS

Basket Case • Black Hole Sun • Come As You Are • Do I Wanna Know? • Gold on the Ceiling • Heaven • How You Remind Me • Kryptonite • No One Knows • Plush • The Pretender • Seven Nation Army • Smooth • Under the Bridge • Yellow Ledbetter.

00244758 Book/Online Audio $19.99

2. REALLY EASY SONGS

All the Small Things • Brain Stew • Californication • Free Fallin' • Helter Skelter • Hey Joe • Highway to Hell • Hurt (Quiet) • I Love Rock 'N Roll • Island in the Sun • Knockin' on Heaven's Door • La Bamba • Oh, Pretty Woman • Should I Stay or Should I Go • Smells Like Teen Spirit.

00244877 Book/Online Audio $19.99

3. ACOUSTIC SONGS

All Apologies • Banana Pancakes • Crash Into Me • Good Riddance (Time of Your Life) • Hallelujah • Hey There Delilah • Ho Hey • I Will Wait • I'm Yours • Iris • More Than Words • No Such Thing • Photograph • What I Got • Wonderwall.

00244709 Book/Online Audio $19.99

4. THE BEATLES

All My Loving • And I Love Her • Back in the U.S.S.R. • Don't Let Me Down • Get Back • A Hard Day's Night • Here Comes the Sun • I Will • In My Life • Let It Be • Michelle • Paperback Writer • Revolution • While My Guitar Gently Weeps • Yesterday.

00244968 Book/Online Audio $19.99

5. BLUES STANDARDS

Baby, What You Want Me to Do • Crosscut Saw • Double Trouble • Every Day I Have the Blues • Going Down • I'm Tore Down • I'm Your Hoochie Coochie Man • If You Love Me Like You Say • Just Your Fool • Killing Floor • Let Me Love You Baby • Messin' with the Kid • Pride and Joy • (They Call It) Stormy Monday (Stormy Monday Blues) • Sweet Home Chicago.

00245090 Book/Online Audio $19.99

6. RED HOT CHILI PEPPERS

The Adventures of Rain Dance Maggie • Breaking the Girl • Can't Stop • Dani California • Dark Necessities • Give It Away • My Friends • Otherside • Road Trippin' • Scar Tissue • Snow (Hey Oh) • Suck My Kiss • Tell Me Baby • Under the Bridge • The Zephyr Song.

00245089 Book/Online Audio $19.99

7. CLASSIC ROCK

Baba O'Riley • Born to Be Wild • Comfortably Numb • Dream On • Fortunate Son • Heartbreaker • Hotel California • Jet Airliner • More Than a Feeling • Old Time Rock & Roll • Rhiannon • Runnin' Down a Dream • Start Me Up • Sultans of Swing • Sweet Home Alabama.

00248381 Book/Online Audio $19.99

8. OZZY OSBOURNE

Bark at the Moon • Close My Eyes Forever • Crazy Train • Dreamer • Goodbye to Romance • I Don't Know • I Don't Wanna Stop • Mama, I'm Coming Home • Miracle Man • Mr. Crowley • No More Tears • Over the Mountain • Perry Mason • Rock 'N Roll Rebel • Shot in the Dark.

00248413 Book/Online Audio $19.99

9. ED SHEERAN

The A Team • All of the Stars • Castle on the Hill • Don't • Drunk • Galway Girl • Give Me Love • How Would You Feel (Paean) • I See Fire • Lego House • Make It Rain • Perfect • Photograph • Shape of You • Thinking Out Loud.

00248439 Book/Online Audio $19.99

www.halleonard.com